JAPAN'S NUCLEAR FUTURE

THE PLUTONIUM DEBATE AND EAST ASIAN SECURITY

**EDITED BY
SELIG S. HARRISON**

A CARNEGIE ENDOWMENT BOOK

© 1996 by the
Carnegie Endowment for International Peace
2400 N Street, N.W.
Washington, D.C. 20037
Tel.(202) 862-7900
Fax.(202) 862-2610

JX
1974.73
J37
1996

Japan's Nuclear Future: The Plutonium Debate and East Asian Security
(ISBN 0-87003-065-5/$12.95)
may be ordered from Carnegie's distributor,
The Brookings Institution, Department 029,
Washington, D.C. 20042-0029, USA.
Tel. (202) 797-6258. Fax (202) 797-6004.

Cover and book design: Paddy McLaughlin Concepts & Design.
Cover photo credits: AP/WideWorld Photos (right);
National Space Development Agency of Japan (left).
Printed by Automated Graphic Systems.

Library of Congress Cataloging-in-Publication Data
Japan's nuclear future: the plutonium debate and East Asian security/
edited and with an introductory essay by Selig S. Harrison 128 pp.
"A Carnegie Endowment book."
includes bibliographical references.
ISBN: 0-87003-065-5
1. Nuclear nonproliferation.
2. Nuclear weapons—Government policy—Japan.
3. Plutonium—Government policy—Japan.
4. Japan—Foreign relations.
5. East Asia—National security
I. Harrison, Selig S.
JX1974.73.J37 1996   96-25602
327.1`74—dc20   CIP

CONTENTS

FOREWORD

The end of the Cold War marked the start of a significant debate in Japan over its future security role in Asia, its contribution to United Nations peacekeeping efforts, and its policies on global and regional arms control and non-proliferation issues. This debate is closely linked with the ongoing effort by the United States and Japan to adapt their security relationship to the changing needs of the post–Cold War period.

As part of a broader effort to promote dialogue on key issues affecting the U.S.–Japan relationship, the Carnegie Endowment sponsored a two-year project on Japan's Role in International Security Affairs during 1994 and 1995 under the direction of Selig S. Harrison. The first two books resulting from this project, *The United States, Japan, and the Future of Nuclear Weapons* and *U.N. Peacekeeping: Japanese and American Perspectives*, were published last year.

This book is an outgrowth of a study group on Japan's Role in Non-Proliferation and Arms Control conducted in 1994 with the support of the Japan–United States Friendship Commission. The group consisted of American specialists and was addressed by Asian specialists who prepared working papers on key topics. Among the wide range of non-proliferation and arms control topics addressed by the study group, the most contentious was the issue of Japan's plutonium-based civilian nuclear-power program and the anxieties this has aroused in neighboring East Asian countries that Japan may become a nuclear-weapons power. The papers in this book present differing perspectives on this critical issue. They were selected from those prepared for the study group and have been revised and updated to take into account new developments. Selig S. Harrison, chairman of the study group and a student of Japanese security affairs for many years, has contributed an introductory essay reviewing the evolution of Japanese nuclear policy and assessing the factors that will affect Japan's nuclear future.

The Endowment would like to express its thanks to the Japan–United States Friendship Commission for the support that made this book possible and to the W. Alton Jones Foundation, the John Merck Fund, the United States–Japan Foundation, and the Center for Global Partnership for their support of other aspects of the project on Japan's Role in International Security Affairs.

The views expressed in this book are solely those of the authors.

Morton I. Abramowitz, *President*
Carnegie Endowment for International Peace

PART 1
OVERVIEW

JAPAN AND NUCLEAR WEAPONS

SELIG S. HARRISON

The most widely read novel in South Korea in recent years has been *The Rose of Sharon Has Blossomed*, a three-volume saga in which North and South Korea cooperate in developing nuclear weapons that save the South in a war with Japan. Sixteen months after publication of the trilogy in October 1994, the same month in which the United States reached its nuclear freeze agreement with Pyongyang, more than 1.3 million people had bought all three volumes, an unprecedented phenomenon in South Korean literary history.[1]

In a plot that mixes elements of historical fact with larger doses of fiction, the novel centers on a Korean-born American nuclear physicist who masterminds a secret South Korean nuclear program during the regime of the late President Park Chung Hee. The CIA, learning of the program, arranges to have the physicist killed in an auto accident. Before his death, using $65 million supplied by Park, he buys 80 kilograms of plutonium from India with the help of an Indian scientist who had been his roommate during U.S. college days. He hides the plutonium in a stone statue of an elephant in the South Korean presidential compound, sharing the secret of its location only with the Indian scientist. There it remains until the Indian reveals the hiding place to a South Korean journalist investigating rumors of a CIA hand in the auto accident.

The journalist, a fervent nationalist who dreams of reviving Park's nuclear program, persuades a fictitious later president that the South and the North must pool their plutonium and missile know-how in order to prepare for an inevitable confrontation with a nuclear-armed Japan. This time, the carefully camouflaged North-South project in the rugged South Korean Taebaek mountains is not detected by American intelligence. Eventually, Japan, alarmed by growing South Korean trade competition, does provoke a war, charging Korean incursions in contested Takeshima island. As Japanese bombers head toward Pohang, the South's major industrial center, Seoul demonstrates its nuclear capability with a missile attack that obliterates an uninhabited Japanese island. Tokyo ignominiously backs down.

The title of the novel—*The Rose of Sharon Has Blossomed*—is the code name for the North-South nuclear program. It is also the name of a popular children's refrain celebrating liberation from Japanese colonialism. South Korea's national flower is called the Rose of Sharon because it resembles the Biblical flower described in the Song of Solomon.

The most important element of historical fact in the plot is that Park Chung Hee did initiate a secret nuclear program in 1971 and was able to carry it forward without detection for three years. In 1975, armed with conclusive intelligence findings, the United States pressured Park to stop the program or face the termination of U.S. military support for the South. The program was revived during the Roh Tae Woo regime in 1991 and soon discontinued once again under U.S. pressure.[2]

It is also true that there was a distinguished Korean-born American nuclear physicist, Lee Hwi So, who died in an auto accident in 1977. An expert on the transmutation of atomic particles, Lee, who directed theoretical physics at the Fermi National Laboratory, was described by *Physics Today* after his death as "one of the world's leading physicists working on the theory of elementary particles."[3] No evidence has surfaced that he helped Park's nuclear program or that his death was not accidental. But his supposed role, and the CIA's complicity in his death, dominate the *Rose of Sharon* and an earlier biography and novel about Lee's life.[4]

What has made the impact of the *Rose of Sharon* so powerful is the widespread and growing fear in South Korea that the prospect of a nuclear-armed Japan is not fantasy but an ever more plausible real-world danger. In the eyes of its East Asian neighbors, Japan is systematically perfecting its capacity to make nuclear weapons overnight by developing independent plutonium-reprocessing and uranium-enrichment capabilities as part of its civilian nuclear program. North Korea, describing Japan as an "associate member of the nuclear club," contrasts its own agreement in 1994 to freeze its reprocessing facilities with Japan's determined pursuit of nuclear independence. China finds evidence of Japan's nuclear ambitions not only in its plutonium accumulation but also in its development of sophisticated rockets for its space program that could be converted to intermediate and intercontinental-range missiles.

Japan insists that its nuclear program is motivated solely by economic and energy-security considerations. Emphasizing energy security, Japanese officials point to forecasts that the world's oil will run out within four or five decades and its uranium soon thereafter. Instead of relying on imported energy sources, they say, Japan is playing it safe by developing its own autonomous nuclear fuel cycle, complete with a reprocessing capability and fast-breeder reactors that can burn plutonium to produce electricity while generating—"breeding"—still more plutonium. Moreover, they argue, memories of Hiroshima and Nagasaki make the nuclear option abhorrent and unacceptable for most Japanese, and it is settled national policy that the nation will not possess or manufacture nuclear weapons or permit their introduction by the United States in carrying out the Japan–U.S. Security Treaty.

In strategic terms, Japanese spokesmen maintain, Japan rules out nuclear weapons because a densely populated island nation located so close to most of its conceivable enemies would be peculiarly vulnerable to a preemptive nuclear attack. Equally important, they add, Japanese business leaders fear that nuclearization would have disastrous economic consequences, jeopardizing access to foreign markets and investment opportunities.

Despite these disclaimers, however, suspicions of Japanese intentions remain undiminished in neighboring countries, especially in South Korea. An influential minority of nationalist intellectuals and political leaders in the South argue that President Roh Tae Woo should never have concluded his 1991 denuclearization agreement with Pyongyang, which prohibits reprocessing by both North and South. In this view, it would have been enough to require safeguards barring the diversion of plutonium for military purposes—leaving the North and South alike free to pursue reprocessing for civilian use, just as Japan is doing, while at the same time acquiring the option of a weapons program.

Defenders of the 1991 agreement argue that the ban on reprocessing was an unavoidable necessity in the context of a divided Korea in which North Korea was on the verge of developing a nuclear-weapons capability. Nationalist critics, blaming American pressure for the 1991 accord, respond that the United States had repeatedly blocked South Korean efforts to acquire reprocessing facilities long before evidence of a possible North Korean nuclear-weapons program emerged. Significantly, both defenders and critics serve notice that a unified Korea will demand the same treatment enjoyed by Japan and will seek a new understanding with the United States and the International Atomic Energy Agency (IAEA) superseding the 1991 accord.

Opposition to the Japanese plutonium program has been growing within Japan itself in parallel with the concern in neighboring countries, especially since a serious accident at the Monju fast-breeder reactor that led to its shutdown in January 1996. An official cover-up of the accident has damaged public trust in the management of nuclear facilities, prompting demands for a reappraisal of Japanese nuclear policy.

This book presents the case for the Japanese plutonium program by one of its most respected proponents, Atsuyuki Suzuki; the arguments advanced against it by a leading Japanese critic, Jinzaburo Takagi; and a South Korean perspective by Taewoo Kim, a prominent non-government nuclear specialist. The central issue posed by Kim and Takagi alike is whether Japanese leaders have developed their nuclear program from the start with the conscious intention of acquiring a militarily applicable nuclear capability, or as Suzuki contends, have pursued it solely for economic, energy-security, and environmental reasons. I have studied this issue over a period of three decades, beginning with the crucial 1968–1972 period, when I lived in Japan as Northeast Asia Bureau Chief of the *Washington Post*. It was during this period that Japan began an intensive and protracted debate over whether, and on what terms, it should sign and ratify the Treaty on the Non-Proliferation of Nuclear Weapons (NPT).

I will begin by reviewing this debate in detail. The evidence presented here, some of it published in English for the first time, shows that many Japanese leaders did want to keep a nuclear weapons option open and have promoted a plutonium-based autonomous nuclear fuel cycle not only for the stated reasons but also because it can be readily converted to a military nuclear program. Against this background, I will assess the technical options open to Japan should it choose to utilize its nuclear and space capabilities for military purposes. I will then discuss the post-Cold War reappraisal of security policy now taking place in Japan in the context of the stalemate in global efforts to wind down nuclear weapons and of President Clinton's 1996 statement justifying the use of the atomic bomb at Hiroshima. Finally, I will consider the factors likely to determine whether Japan decides to become a nuclear weapons power and will suggest four new departures in American policy that will minimize this possibility. The bottom line of this analysis is that the continuance of the American nuclear umbrella over Japan will not, in itself, assure a non-nuclear Japan unless it is accompanied by meaningful U.S. and Russian steps leading to a global process of nuclear disarmament embracing China.

TO SIGN OR NOT TO SIGN: THE NPT CONTROVERSY

J apan was one of the last countries to sign the NPT in 1970 and finally ratified it six years later only after the United States promised not to interfere with Tokyo's pursuit of independent reprocessing capabilities in its civilian nuclear–power program. When the United States first circulated drafts of the projected treaty in early 1966, Vice-Foreign Minister Takeso Shimoda told a press conference that "Japan cannot agree to such a big power–centered approach, implying as it does that the nuclear powers would not be required to reduce their capabilities or stockpile, while the non-nuclear powers would be barred in this treaty from having nuclear weapons."[5] Shimoda's comments reflected widespread sentiment in the ruling Liberal Democratic Party that Japan should not foreclose its nuclear option, and that it was time for the Japanese public to get over the trauma of Hiroshima. The party's secretary general, Takeo Fukuda, aroused a storm when he said on December 14, 1967, that "the majority of the Liberal Democrats see the need to outgrow the 'nuclear allergy.'" Prime Minister Eisaku Sato made a similar statement ten days later. Four opposition parties led by the Buddhist Komeito promptly announced a campaign "to counter the government effort to mollify the nation's anti-nuclear weapons sentiments and engender an atmosphere favorable to these weapons."[6]

The controversy over the NPT was intensified by a parallel debate over the terms for the projected return of Okinawa to Japan. Ironically, at the same time that U.S. arms control officials were promoting the NPT, the Pentagon was seeking Japanese assurances that the United States could continue to keep nuclear weapons in its Okinawan bases if it gave the island back to Japan. Prime Minister Sato had made no secret of his readiness to give the United States such assurances. But he faced strong public sentiment against risking involvement in an "American war" in Korea or elsewhere in Asia that could well involve nuclear weapons. North Korea's seizure of the Pueblo spy ship on January 23, 1968, and the subsequent deployment of the aircraft carrier *Enterprise* from a Japanese port sharpened these ever-present anxieties. On February 5, 1968, Sato was forced to make his Diet pledge, known as the Three Non-Nuclear Principles, that Japan "will not manufacture or possess nuclear weapons or allow their introduction into this country," and on November 24, 1971, the Diet formalized this policy in a resolution.

Unknown to the Japanese public at the time, Sato commissioned a secret study on Japanese nuclear policy in late 1967 by an advisory group consisting of key government officials and scholars specializing in foreign policy and strategic issues. Political scientist Michio Royama, who revealed the existence of this study in 1994, said that Sato had specifically asked the group to examine whether it was possible and desirable for Japan to develop independent nuclear forces. The study pointed out that there were "no technical impediments" to such forces, Royama said, and that the plutonium stocks resulting from its civilian nuclear-power program would give Japan the option of making nuclear weapons. But it concluded that a nuclear-weapons program was undesirable because it would cost too much, would alarm neighboring countries, and would not have the majority support of the Japanese public. Moreover, in order to sustain American cooperation in developing its civilian nuclear-power program, the report added, Japan would have to sign the NPT.[7] Significantly, discussing the study with an American journalist, Royama observed that the costs of making a nuclear arsenal, which seemed forbidding in 1967, "would not be a factor for Japan today." While he still opposes going nuclear, he said, "we don't know what the future holds. Let's not close that path."[8]

The fact that its civilian nuclear-power program would give Japan a built-in weapons option was explicitly recognized in a mid-1968 study published by the Security Research Council, a think tank sponsored by the Japanese Defense Agency. Looking ahead to Japanese defense problems in the 1970s, the study said that Japan could make 20 to 30 nuclear weapons per year if its civilian nuclear reactors discontinued power generation and were devoted entirely to the production of fissile plutonium 239.[9] Similarly, eight months later, former Prime Minister Nobusuke Kishi declared that "when our standard of technology of peaceful utilization of nuclear energy is increased, it will be a great help in case our country promotes nuclear weapons."[10]

"WE WILL KEEP THE ECONOMIC AND TECHNICAL POTENTIAL"

The importance of keeping the nuclear-weapons option open was spelled out in a policy planning study on Japan's foreign policy challenges in the coming decade prepared by the Foreign Ministry for internal government use in early 1969. Portions of the study were leaked to *Mainichi* in 1994 by one of the officials who had been involved. "For the time being," said the study, "we will maintain the policy of not possessing nuclear weapons. However, regardless of joining the NPT or not, we will keep the economic and technical potential for the production of nuclear weapons, while seeing to it that Japan will not be interfered with in this regard."[11] Another, more sensitive passage of the study not quoted in *Mainichi* added that "we will educate the public that policies concerning nuclear weapons should be based on cost-benefit calculations with regard to international economic and political factors. Thus, we will seek to avoid needless domestic confusion should tactical nuclear weapons be introduced in a future emergency."[12]

By March 1969, mounting domestic pressures had forced Sato to declare that Japan would accept the return of Okinawa only after the U.S. nuclear weapons there were removed. The Pentagon gradually abandoned its efforts to obtain nuclear storage facilities or a two-key, Japanese-American nuclear arrangement as part of the Okinawa reversion package but did seek to obtain private assurances from Japanese leaders that U.S. nuclear weapons could be reintroduced to the island in an emergency. Six weeks before the Okinawa agreement was signed, General Earle G. Wheeler, Chairman of the Joint Chiefs of Staff, stopped off in Tokyo for talks with Sato, explaining to journalists in an off-the-record briefing that he had been "satisfied" by his assurances on the nuclear issue:

> We will have to take a hard look at our needs on Okinawa, and they will have to take a look at their attitudes. If you're willing to have a nuclear-powered merchant ship, and a nuclear reac-

9

tor, you have to look at the question of nuclear weapons also. Whether we like it or not, we live in the nuclear age. Whether we like it or not, the Chicoms are developing a nuclear force. Do we want to extend our nuclear umbrella forever over Japan, India and other countries? On balance, I'm against their having nuclear weapons, though. There are other ways.[13]

On November 21, 1969, Prime Minister Sato and President Nixon issued a communiqué in Washington confirming that the United States would return Okinawa. In addition to the publicly revealed text, the communiqué had a secret Agreed Minute that was disclosed in 1994 by Kei Wakaizumi, a Japanese scholar who accompanied Sato to Washington. Even the public text carefully left the door open for a change in the ban on the introduction of nuclear weapons. The President expressed his "deep understanding" of the "particular sentiment of the Japanese people against nuclear weapons and the policy of the Japanese government reflecting such sentiment." But the key word "policy" underlined the fact that the Three Non-Nuclear Principles were not embodied in a binding law or treaty. In the Agreed Minute, Nixon was more explicit, declaring that "in time of great emergency the United States Government will require the re-entry of nuclear weapons and transit rights in Okinawa with prior consultation with the government of Japan" as well as "the standby retention and activation in time of great emergency of existing nuclear storage locations." Sato explicitly accepted this caveat.[14]

Less than three weeks later, Sato underlined his own ambivalent attitude on the nuclear issue, sarcastically observing in an address before top leaders of the Keidanren business federation that:

> We seem to be unable to possess a complete system of armament in our country, since we were the ones who were "nuclear-baptized" and the Japanese people have a special sentiment against nuclear weapons. It's regrettable, indeed, but that's where we stand just now. . . . Let me say this so that no one can misunderstand me: I do not regard it as a complete system of defense if we cannot possess nuclear weapons in the era of nuclear weapons. I will, nevertheless, adhere faithfully to the pledge I have made to the people. We will not possess, manufacture or permit the introduction of nuclear weapons; but this being so, it is inevitable, then, that we must seek our security under the U.S. nuclear umbrella.[15]

It was galling to the pro-nuclear elements that Washington should press them to keep the Japanese nuclear option open while urging them, at the same time, to sign the NPT and trust in the U.S. nuclear shield. Until West Germany signed the treaty in December, 1969, Japan stalled in the hope that it might be possible to fudge a decision indefinitely. But the Bonn decision and the prospect that the treaty would come into force within a matter of months brought the issue to a head. When Japan did sign the treaty on February 3, 1970, the Foreign Ministry expressed open doubts that foreshadowed the ensuing six-year delay in ratification. In a striking departure from the cautious understatement marking most official Japanese pronouncements, the eleven-point Foreign Ministry declaration pointedly declared that "this treaty permits only the present nuclear-weapon states to possess nuclear weapons. This discrimination should ultimately be made to disappear through the elimination of nuclear weapons by all the nuclear-weapon states from their national arsenals." The statement specifically noted that Article Ten gave each signatory "the right to withdraw from the treaty if it decides that extraordinary events . . . have jeopardized its supreme interests."

Warning that the treaty must "in no way subject non-nuclear weapons states to discriminatory treatment . . . in the peaceful use of nuclear energy," the statement conditioned ratification on the outcome of negotiations with the IAEA on a safeguards agreement. For the next six years, until the very eve of ratification, Japan bargained with the IAEA for what the statement called the "maximum use" of the "national self-inspection" privileges enjoyed by the European atomic energy consortium, EURATOM.[16]

Once a consensus had been reached to sign the NPT, Japan's most outspoken advocate of nuclear weapons, Defense Agency director Yasuhiro Nakasone, cleared the way for his subsequent rise to the Prime Ministership by reversing his position. "A triangular stalemate is developing between the United States, the Soviet Union and China," he declared in March 1970, "and in this stalemate we will find our security without joining the nuclear club ourselves."[17] However, just three months later, Nakasone bitterly lamented the fact that:

> The two superpowers seem determined to maintain their dominance in nuclear technology in general and its military application in particular. . . . Both the 1963 partial nuclear test ban

treaty and the current nuclear non-proliferation pact are primarily designed—even if covertly—to preempt, or rather deter, both Japan and West Germany from acquiring nuclear arms and thereby undermining the basis of US–Soviet nuclear hegemony.

China opted for 'going nuclear without pants.' Japan, on the other hand, has remained non-nuclear, preferring to be decently dressed. Only history will be able to determine who was wiser. Whether wise or foolish, Japan should not forget . . . that nuclear arms policies tacitly are a reflection of a US–Soviet agreement regarding their respective share of the trophies of World War II.[18]

In an unprecedented 98-page *White Paper*, Nakasone's Defense Agency declared in October 1970, that:

There are nihilistic feelings about nuclear weapons prevailing among the people . . . Japan should not acquire weapons which pose a threat to other countries, such as intercontinental ballistic missiles (ICBMs) and strategic bombers. As for defensive nuclear weapons, it would be possible in a legal sense to possess small-yield, tactical, purely defensive nuclear weapons without violating the Constitution. In view of the danger of inviting adverse foreign reactions and large-scale war, we will follow the policy of not acquiring nuclear weapons at present.[19]

Implying as it did that the "policy" pursued "at present" could change, the *White Paper* provoked bitter protests from anti-nuclear leaders, who charged that the Pentagon and the Defense Agency were plotting a "two-key" nuclear strategy to counter emerging Chinese missile capabilities.

A revealing hint of the policy struggles within the Japanese government during the decade of debate over the NPT was offered by nuclear scientist Hiromi Arisawa, often called the father of nuclear power in Japan, who served as a member and then chairman of the Atomic Energy Commission for 17 years.[20] When he retired in 1972, Arisawa told an *Asahi* interviewer that "we were pressed repeatedly for permission to do basic research on how to make an atomic bomb. They tried to persuade us to do so by saying that such research was permissible under the Constitution. Naturally, I always refused."[21] Arisawa did not specify who "they" were, but it is noteworthy that during part of his tenure, Nakasone was the Minister of Science and Technology, with jurisdiction over the nuclear program.

12

It was not just Sato and Nakasone, both declared pro-nuclear hawks, who kept the nuclear debate alive by emphasizing the distinction between strategic and tactical nuclear weapons. Prime Minister Kakuei Tanaka, reaffirming Sato's Three Non-Nuclear Principles on March 20, 1973, added that "while we are not able to have offensive nuclear weapons, it is not a question of saying that we will have no nuclear weapons at all."[22] In its 1980 *White Paper*, the Defense Agency once again noted, as it did in 1970, that defensive nuclear weapons would not violate the Constitution, specifically mentioning Nike-Hercules air defense missiles and 203 mm howitzers.[23]

Japan did finally ratify the NPT in 1976 after protracted negotiations with the IAEA and the United States. The IAEA accepted a safeguards agreement that limited its inspection to "strategic points" in the nuclear fuel cycle. Equally important, the Nixon and Ford Administrations gave assurances that the United States would not interfere with Japan's acquisition of plutonium and its development of an autonomous fuel cycle. Under the 1968 Japan–U.S. nuclear cooperation agreement, the United States provided the enriched uranium used in Japanese reactors. Japan had to get case-by-case U.S. approval in order to have the resulting spent fuel reprocessed in Europe and to build its own reprocessing facilities and breeder reactors. As Japan had feared, once it ratified the NPT, the United States promptly reneged on its promises not to interfere with the plutonium program. Invoking the 1978 Non-Proliferation Act, the Carter Administration pushed Japan to abandon its plans for an autonomous nuclear program and to rely instead solely on U.S.–supplied uranium to operate its reactors. As Ryukichi Imai has recalled, "it was a bitter irony for us that American officials were telling us not to produce plutonium at the very time that the US was optimizing its nuclear weapons."[24] Japan successfully resisted American pressures during the Carter period. Then Ronald Reagan went even further than Nixon and Ford to accommodate Japanese wishes, agreeing in 1987 to a revised nuclear accord that gave blanket American approval in advance for Japan to reprocess U.S.–origin spent fuel during the ensuing thirty years.[25]

THE UNITED STATES AND THE "NUCLEAR ALLERGY"

In contrast with U.S. apprehensions in recent years concerning the possibility of a nuclear-armed Japan, the Nixon Administration had an ambivalent attitude that did indeed encourage Japanese hawks to pursue the idea of tactical nuclear weapons. Under the "total force" strategic concept initiated by Defense Secretary Melvin R. Laird, the United States could reduce its worldwide commitments only if there were allies ready to play a compensating role at their own expense, if possible under overall U.S. control. In its application to Japan, the "total force" concept rested on an underlying feeling that the United States had been overly generous with Japan, providing a free ride in defense that merited gratitude in the form of equitable Japanese trade policies and, above all, military burden-sharing. Increasingly, the U.S. drive for burden-sharing carried with it a readiness to call Japan's bluff: If Tokyo would not help pay for the U.S. deterrent, the United States should not be afraid to see Japan go it alone militarily, even to the extent of nuclear weaponry. This approach assumed that, given the preponderance of American power and Japanese dependence on the world economy, Japan would have no choice but to remain on the U.S. side in the power struggle with the Soviet Union and might even agree, in time, to a two-key nuclear arrangement under partial U.S. control.

From the Pentagon perspective, the Japanese public remained just as nuclear-allergic as ever to each and every nuclear-powered U.S. ship or submarine entering Japanese harbors, not to mention the nuclear-armed aircraft and naval vessels that were generally suspected to be transiting in and out of Japanese ports without public knowledge. The U.S. Navy, in particular, found it exasperating to be treated with undisguised suspicion by an ally and had never forgiven Japan for the uproar over alleged nuclear leakage in a 1968 incident at Sasebo involving a U.S. nuclear submarine. Tensions grew in Washington between the Pentagon, on the one hand, and the State Department, allied with the Atomic Energy Commission, over how far to push the Japanese for more thoroughgoing military cooperation with the United States, particularly with respect to access by nuclear-powered vessels.

The issue of nuclear access to Japan had assumed a special importance in the eyes of Pentagon planners seeking to implement the total-force strategy. In his annual defense report to Congress in March 1971, Defense Secretary Laird had given increased emphasis to the concept of "theater nuclear deterrence" as the key to compensating for the limitations on the U.S. military posture imposed by the new "one and one-half war" strategy and the Nixon Doctrine. Both Laird and the President emphasized that the administration's policy of "truly flexible response" permitted the use of a "full range of options" without regard to the level of conflict selected by possible enemies. In effect, Laird proposed to compensate for the reduction of conventional capabilities in Asia with a more credible threat to use tactical nuclear weapons. But this presupposed, in turn, that the total-force idea could really be put into practice through "a new basis of cooperation between us and our allies which takes into account their growing capabilities."[26]

In Japanese eyes, the report left little doubt that, even in their hypothetical war games, Pentagon planners were no longer thinking seriously in terms of an ICBM exchange in defense of allies. The underlying objective of theater deterrence was clearly to limit the U.S. nuclear defense of allies to tactical nuclear weapons and to confine any nuclear damage to the territory of U.S. allies or their enemies.

Moreover, in addition to its new note of ambiguity on ICBM protection, the Laird strategy raised questions in Tokyo by sketching an ideal model of theater deterrence in which allies were depicted as having their own tactical nuclear capabilities. There was no direct mention of Japan in this connection, either pointing toward nuclear weaponry for Tokyo or specifically ruling this out. However, the inability of Japan to play a tactical nuclear role à la West Germany was treated, by implication, as an unfortunate anomaly. Summarizing the principles underlying the total-force concept, Laird drew a sharp distinction. In deterring strategic nuclear war, he said, "primary reliance will continue to be placed in U.S. strategic deterrent forces." By contrast, he declared, with an approving nod toward the NATO nuclear partnership, "in deterring theater nuclear war, the U.S. also has primary responsibility, but certain of our allies are able to share this responsibility by virtue of their own nuclear capabilities."[27]

THE PENTAGON SUGGESTS A
JAPANESE NUCLEAR ROLE

The Laird report contained another passage that was to assume added significance when the nuclear issue arose during his contro-

15

versial July 1971 visit to Japan. While U.S. nuclear superiority could "contribute significantly" to deterring aggression by Peking, Laird observed, the American deterrent would be "strengthened further with an area ballistic missile defense effective against small attacks." This was an allusion to a U.S. Navy proposal for a nuclear-armed Seabased Anti-Ballistic Missile Intercept System (SABMIS) as a complement to the Safeguard ABM program. The $2 billion plan envisaged a fleet of up to forty armored ships equipped with Spartan nuclear anti-missile missiles and a miniaturized Nike-X radar and computer apparatus. The proponents of SABMIS were only too aware in early 1971 that the Strategic Arms Limitation Talks then under way were expected to rule out sea-based as well as land-based American ABM systems. A future SABMIS in Asia would have to be Japanese, possibly based on American technological help purchased from American defense industries.

On July 5, 1971, the second day of his Tokyo visit, Laird outlined the case for a nuclear Japan at a meeting with six ranking American embassy officials, conducting what several of those present described as a "Socratic dialogue." His personal position was not stated, as such, but the clear impression left was that he had been testing his own views. Embassy officials were not surprised, therefore, when Laird's spokesman, Jerry Friedheim, later to become Assistant Secretary of Defense, spelled out what the Secretary had in mind at a background briefing for American and British journalists on July 7. Friedheim pointed out that Japan was likely to face a radically new strategic environment as a result of the impending SALT I agreement, since the accord could lead to a reduced U.S. nuclear posture in the Pacific while China would be free to develop its missile strength unchecked. The ICBM threat to the United States from Beijing would still be "decades" away, and the United States would feel less directly threatened than ever before by Moscow. Tokyo could choose to help the United States to maintain the nuclear deterrent in the Pacific by abandoning its inhibitions with respect to nuclear access, by providing direct financial support, and by building expanded conventional naval forces. Or it could develop its own defensive nuclear weapons, he said, either as a two-key supplement to the U.S. nuclear umbrella or under independent Japanese control. "They might want to go for ABMs on ships," Friedheim said, alluding to the SABMIS idea that Laird had mentioned in his defense report to Congress.[28]

The emergence of a new American attitude on the nuclear issue was soon confirmed when a White House official told *Nihon Keizai* editor Yasuo Takeyama in November 1971 that "if Japan wishes, the U.S. is prepared to provide Japan nuclear warheads or the know-how to manufacture nuclear warheads."[29] Changing American attitudes with respect to a nuclear Japan were most forcefully suggested when President Nixon made his controversial statement in January 1972 that "I think it will be a safer world and a better world if we have a strong, healthy United States, Europe, Soviet Union, China, Japan, each balancing the other, not playing one against the other, an even balance."[30] This marked a change from the careful reference in his Kansas City speech, six months earlier, to "five great economic superpowers." This time, the economic qualifier was missing, and the inference was clearly drawn in Tokyo that the balance could not be "even" unless both Japan and Europe were nuclear.

Japanese hawks reacted coolly to the Nixon concept, fearful that the balance would not really be "even" and that Japan would be a junior partner in a two-key arrangement, forced to play the U.S. game in matters involving the Soviet Union and China. For advocates of nuclear weapons in Japan, the very purpose of going nuclear would be to assert independence from the United States, and Nixon, in particular, had become a target of nationalist resentment. In Japanese eyes, Nixon symbolized cavalier American policies that took Japan for granted, especially in trade disputes. Nixon's unilateral overtures to China, bypassing Japan, provoked a sharp reaction typified by Kiichi Miyazawa, then recently retired as Minister of International Trade and Industry and later to become Prime Minister. In December 1971, Miyazawa told an interviewer:

> Recent events have been influenced by distinctions between 'first-rate' and 'second-rate' nations, using nuclear capabilities and atomic stockpiles as yardsticks . . . If the major nations of the world who have nuclear capabilities try to be too assertive and push Japan around too much and too far, they may run the risk of opening up what they most want to avoid.

> There is already a body of opinion in Japan which feels that dependence on the US nuclear umbrella is basically incompatible with our national sovereignty. When the coming generations assume a greater role in the society, they may want to choose the lesser of two evils and opt to build their own

umbrella instead of renting their neighbor's, if only to satisfy their desire to be their own masters. This may become likelier as time passes and memories of Hiroshima and Nagasaki recede.[31]

THE NUCLEAR OPTION

The controversy surrounding Japan's reliance on a plutonium-based nuclear program has focused to date primarily on two issues: whether or not large plutonium stocks will accumulate, and whether reactor-grade plutonium can be used for nuclear weapons. Takagi's compelling projections in these pages of an accumulation ranging from 11 to 25 tons by the turn of the century, and from 50 to 80 tons by the year 2010, call into question Suzuki's assurances that supply and demand will be kept in balance. Moreover, even official projections indicate that buffer stocks of 5 tons are likely at any one time. Estimates by independent experts indicate that from 1 to 8 kilograms of plutonium—depending on the grade of plutonium, the specific weapon design, and the desired explosive yield involved—is sufficient fissile material for a fission (as distinct from fusion) weapon with a yield in the range of one to 20 kilotons. A relatively simple medium-technology pure fission weapon with a maximum probable yield of about 20 kilotons could be constructed with a little less than 4 kilograms of reactor-grade plutonium. Using this estimate as a benchmark, Japan's projected 5-ton buffer stocks would represent the potential for about 1,000 weapons, allowing for losses in the production process.[32]

The expert judgments cited in Appendices A and B leave little doubt that reactor-grade plutonium can be used for weapons, though it has "disadvantages" compared with plutonium produced expressly for military purposes. However, if Japan should decide to go nuclear, it would not have to rely on reactor-grade plutonium. Five other routes to a weapons program would also be available:

- Producing weapon-grade plutonium in reactors now used exclusively for generating electricity by shutting them down more frequently for refueling, thereby reducing the irradiation level ("burnup") of the fuel to weapon-grade;

- Upgrading reactor-grade plutonium to weapon-grade, or producing highly enriched uranium, through use of a laser-isotope process now under experimental development at the government-operated Institute for Physical and Chemical Research at Osaka University;

- Converting the centrifuges in its uranium-enrichment facilities at Rokasshomura from the production of low-enriched uranium (4.5 percent U-235) to highly enriched uranium usable in compact nuclear weapons (greater than 80 percent U-235).

- Separating the super-grade plutonium produced in the natural uranium "blankets" of its Joyo and Monju fast-breeder reactors, which has a higher degree of purity than the plutonium used in U.S. nuclear weapons; and

- Producing weapon-grade plutonium in a reactor specifically configured for the purpose.

Producing weapon-grade plutonium in reactors designed for electric power generation would require frequent and costly shutdowns and would thus interfere with efficient electric power production. Moreover, Japan is dependent on those reactors to meet its electricity needs.

The laser-isotope process has already been successfully tested at the laboratory level, and the technology may have commercial uses in addition to its military utility. While the economics of a production-scale plant for the commercial production of low-enriched uranium fuel has yet to be demonstrated, development programs are under way in the United States and France as well as in Japan.

Similarly, conversion of other enrichment technologies, such as centrifuges, for the production of highly enriched uranium would not be technically difficult. But nuclear weapons made with highly enriched uranium are bulkier than those made from plutonium. This difference could make it more difficult to develop missile warheads that are both powerful and compact.

Perhaps the most attractive option in the event of a weapons program would be separating the high-purity supergrade plutonium from the breeder blankets. This plutonium could then be used separately or blended with separated reactor-grade plutonium to create a larger supply of weapon-grade plutonium. The prototype fast-breeder reactor at Monju, which began operating in January 1995, had accumulated an estimated 10 kilograms in its blanket when it was shut down after the sodium leak. When and if it is restored to operation, an additional 70 kilograms per year could be added to this accumulation, depending on the level of production.[33] Even in the event that it is not restored to full operation, its continued use as a research or experimental facility would permit further accumulations of supergrade plutonium. The Joyo experimental fast-breeder reactor had accumulated 40 kilograms in its blankets when the reactor shifted to a new design in 1994 that no longer requires blankets.[34]

In 1967, ten years before Joyo went into operation, Victor Gilinsky, then a RAND Corporation physicist and later a member of the U.S. Nuclear Regulatory Commission, warned that:

> It is an intrinsic property of fast breeders that about half of the plutonium produced by the breeders, the part bred in the outer 'blanket,' will have a rather low content of the troublesome isotope plutonium 240, possibly less than five percent, even when produced in the most economical way. This material can therefore be used for military purposes with particular ease. On the other hand, the plutonium produced from economical operation of thermal reactors contains a relatively high fraction of plutonium 240 and is generally less useful for weapons.[35]

Based on French experience since 1967, Japan's supergrade plutonium would have a plutonium 240 content of only 2-3 percent—compared with 6 percent in U.S. nuclear weapons. The availability of plutonium of this high level of purity, as compared with reactor grade plutonium, would reduce the need to conduct test explosions—a factor of great significance for Japan, with its population density and lack of suitable test sites. Moreover, less of such a pure grade of plutonium would be needed for one nuclear warhead, which would make it easier for Japan to make warheads small enough for advanced cruise missiles and ICBMs. Still another military advantage of supergrade plutonium is that in simple designs it is less susceptible than reactor-grade plutonium to premature detonation resulting from spontaneous fission.

Supergrade plutonium must be separated through reprocessing from the uranium 238 from which it is produced in the breeder blankets. With American technical help, as revealed in a Greenpeace study, [36] Japan is developing a special reprocessing plant, known as the Recycling Equipment Test Facility (RETF), designed expressly to separate supergrade plutonium in conjunction with the existing reprocessing plant at Tokai. The completion of this plant, now scheduled for the year 2000, would greatly reduce the time required for the development of a nuclear-weapons program.

However, it is possible that the Monju reactor accident will lead to delays in the construction of the RETF and conceivably to its eventual cancellation. Japanese plans concerning this sensitive facility will be closely watched in the years ahead.

THE MISSILE OPTION

T he fact that Japan already possesses, or could readily produce, substantial amounts of weapons-grade plutonium and uranium does not, in itself, mean that it could develop a significant nuclear-weapons capability. It is the sophisticated character of the Japanese space program, with its convertibility to missile development, that makes Japan's potential as a nuclear power so formidable. In Tom Clancy's best-selling 1995 novel, *Debt of Honor*, which centers on a secret Japanese nuclear-weapons program, Japan makes its own nuclear warheads and puts them on SS-19 ICBMs purchased from Russia.[37] But the reality is that Japan would not have to rely on any other power for missile technology. With foreign help, Japan has steadily built up its space capabilities. A controversial U.S.–Japan space cooperation agreement that remained in force from 1969 to 1984 embraced significant areas of space technology with military applications. Since the termination of this government-to-government cooperation, Japan has acquired less American technology in sensitive areas such as guidance. But a wide range of space-related private sector cooperation between the two countries has continued with U.S. government encouragement.

Japanese space agencies have successfully tested solid-fueled rocket systems that could be directly converted to intercontinental-range missiles. Both of these systems, the J-1 and the M-5, have a payload and a thrust comparable to that of U.S. ICBMs. John Pike, Director of the Space Policy Project of the Federation of American Scientists, stated that "if converted to ballistic missile applications, the M-5 would seem likely to give Japan an ICBM roughly equivalent to the MX Peacekeeper, the largest currently operational U.S. ICBM, and the J-1 would probably give Japan an ICBM surpassing the performance of a Minuteman 3." The range of the Minuteman 3 is about 8,000 miles, and that of the Peacekeeper, some 7,400. The J-1 was developed by marrying a solid-propellant motor from another successfully-tested liquid-fueled rocket, the H-2, to the upper stages of the MS 32, a precursor of the M-5.

"By firing their existing launch vehicles at long trajectories not suitable for space launches but appropriate for missiles," Pike explained, "Japan could greatly increase the throw-weight of a missile relative to the space launch payload. For example, an intermediate-range missile capable of covering China might have a throw-weight as much as three to five times that of the satellite payload of the space launch vehicle from which it is derived."

Supergrade plutonium is especially suited for the miniaturization of warheads. Since it is a more reliable explosive than grades with less purity, involving less danger of premature detonation, the other components of the warhead could be small and light. Thus, a warhead weighing 150 kilograms, containing 3 kilograms of supergrade, would be suitable for an advanced-model cruise missile with a range of 2,500 kilometers. Similarly, if Japan were to make an ICBM of the Multiple Independently Targetable Re-entry Vehicle (MIRV) type based on technology drawn from the M-5, each warhead would weigh about 350 kilograms, and the missile would be able to carry between five and ten warheads, depending on its range.[38] The M-5 has an orbital payload capacity of 1.8 tons, which would be increased if the missile were fired on a ballistic trajectory. The US Minuteman 3 and MX Peacekeeper, both MIRV-type ICBMs, can carry three and ten warheads respectively.

The Japanese space effort has entailed the development of guidance and re-entry technology that could be applied to a missile program. Advanced guidance techniques were required to place and keep in orbit the unmanned space platform that was launched by the H-2 in 1995 to collect scientific data relating to research in the evolution of the universe. Japanese officials point out that targeting for a ballistic missile would require a much greater degree of precision in re-entry technology than has yet been achieved. But the extent of precision required would depend on whether the missile would be designed for a "counterforce" strategy (i.e., directed at missile silos or other hard targets) or for a "countervalue" (i.e., 'citybusting') strategy. The Orex re-entry vehicle developed for the H-2 demonstrates mastery of the techniques that would be needed in targeting area targets such as cities. Pike estimated that the relevant re-entry technology for this purpose could be perfected "in a matter of months." By contrast, he observed, it would take "three to four years" for Japan to develop the precision in re-entry technology that would be needed for a "counterforce" strategy.

Pointing to "the symbiotic military-civilian nature of space technology," Professor Joan Johnson-Freese of the U.S. Air War College, in her definitive study of the Japanese space program,[39] has recounted the sharp internal conflicts in Washington that accompanied the birth of the U.S. program of space cooperation with Japan in 1969. When Ambassador to Japan U. Alexis Johnson first pushed for such cooperation, he encountered "strong reservations about any such type of agreement" from the Defense Department and the National Aeronautics and Space Agency (NASA). It was only after Johnson became Undersecretary of State for Political Affairs that he was able to get Pentagon and NASA objections "overruled by the National Security Council on the basis that the agreement would be good for overall political relations between Japan and the United States."[40] This opened the way for Japan to license aspects of the technology used in the Thor-Delta missile from McDonnell Douglas to build its "N" series of rockets, with a payload capacity that ultimately reached 350 kilograms. In deference to the Pentagon, however, the Japanese were denied access to the IBM computer on board the Thor-Delta rocket, which was sealed "in a 'black box' because the technology was still used in intercontinental ballistic missiles."[41]

As the implementation of the agreement progressed, Johnson-Freese writes, "US willingness to grant export licenses in many key areas of technology" with military applications, such as "inertial guidance, spacecraft stabilization, and cryogenic propulsion, was sharply curtailed." Nevertheless, by the time the U.S.–Japan space agreement ended in 1984, Japan "had enough experience with rocket technology to develop an autonomous capability." Indeed, the H series, of which the H-2 is a part, was undertaken precisely because successfully developing on its own a launcher capable of carrying such a big payload "would be highly symbolic of 'catching up' with the United States" in space technology.[42] Although U.S. help enabled Japan to build up its space capabilities "more quickly and more easily than would otherwise have been the case," Johnson-Freese told me, "there is no question that they could have achieved their present levels of technology eventually with or without U.S. help."[43]

Both the nuclear and space programs in Japan are governed by explicit legislative restrictions barring their use for military purposes. Both have been 'sold' to the public as sound economic investments that will pay off handsomely sooner or later and will give the country technological independence in these key sectors. The case for plutonium and fast-breeder reactors has been reinforced by the argument that an autonomous nuclear fuel cycle is essential for national energy security. At the same time, as the record cited here shows, the priority accorded to both the nuclear and space programs by a succession of Japanese governments has reflected a clear recognition on the part of many key bureaucrats and political leaders that these programs give Japan the critical elements of a nuclear-weapons capability.

Prime Minister Tsutomu Hata explicitly acknowledged this capability when a hawkish Liberal Democratic Party Diet member told him in a closed committee hearing that Japan should "confirm to other nations that it can produce nuclear weapons but is refraining from doing so out of respect for the NPT." Hata's response that he "agrees absolutely" prompted inquiries from reporters, whereupon Hata said that "it's certainly the case that Japan has the capability to possess nuclear weapons but has not made them."[44]

AFTER THE COLD WAR: REASSESSING SECURITY POLICY

The very fact that this capability exists made it unnecessary for advocates of nuclear weapons to keep pressing their case once Japan finally decided to ratify the NPT in 1976. During the final years of the Cold War, the public debate over nuclear policy gradually subsided, and the anti-nuclear forces reestablished the national consensus that Japan should remain non-nuclear.

This consensus rests on the assumption that Japan will continue to have U.S. nuclear protection. Yet even at the height of the Cold War, many Japanese defense specialists questioned the reliability of the U.S. nuclear deterrent. An authoritative study concluded in 1966 that it would be "highly unthinkable" for the United States to risk a nuclear exchange with Russia or China for the sake of Japan. The Communist powers could use Japan as a hostage to deter an American attack, the study said, and there would be "little practical meaning" in the destruction of Communist cities after "Tokyo and Osaka had been turned into a second Hiroshima and Nagasaki."[45] Pro-nuclear hawks have viewed the U.S. nuclear deterrent as a temporary expedient, offering a modicum of political and psychological protection in dealing with nuclear-armed neighbors pending the day, as Sato put it, when Japanese "are able to possess a complete system of armament in our country," deploying "nuclear weapons in the era of nuclear weapons." Conversely, in the eyes of the anti-nuclear majority, the U.S. nuclear umbrella has a more immutable, transcendent value precisely because it provides a rationale for keeping Japan non-nuclear.

Since the end of the Cold War, Japanese doubts concerning the credibility of the U.S. nuclear umbrella have been carefully nurtured by proponents of an independent nuclear capability, who point to U.S.–Japanese trade conflicts and domestic U.S. pressures for the reduction of U.S. forces in Asia. In the post–Cold War security environment, the hawks argue, American and Japanese interests are diverging, since the United States is no longer directly threatened by China and Russia, while Japan faces a wide range of potential political, economic, and security conflicts with Beijing, Moscow, and possibly Pyongyang.

The case for nuclear weapons focuses in particular on Chinese deployments of medium-range missiles with nuclear warheads—in 1996, 10 DF-4s with a range of 4,750 miles and 60 DF-3s with a range of 2,800 miles—as well as growing conventional power-projection capabilities. Japanese nuclear weapons advocates argue that China will sooner or later seek to assert regional dominance in Asia at Japan's expense, and that Beijing's aggressive intentions have already been foreshadowed by military muscle-flexing in the South China Sea and the East China Sea. The U.S. policy of calculated ambiguity during the March 1996 Chinese military exercises in the Taiwan Strait is cited as evidence that the United States cannot be relied upon for protection in the event of a nuclear threat from China. Similarly, the U.S. effort to promote a jointly developed theater missile-defense system in East Asia, with Japan footing most of the bill, has added to Japanese concern about the credibility of the U.S. deterrent. Although the United States depicts the new system as an adjunct to continued nuclear protection, the prevailing impression in Japan is that the concept of theater missile defense, like the earlier Laird concept of theater nuclear deterrence, is attractive to the United States as a way of phasing out the Cold War concept of extended deterrence.

Hawkish Japanese defense specialists warn explicitly that a

rupture in the U.S. alliance would mean a nuclear-armed Japan. For example, Hisahiko Okazaki, a former Ambassador to Saudi Arabia and Thailand, declared that "if Japan had to do everything for its own defense, it would go nuclear. This would come from necessity, not from the revival of militarism."[46]

By contrast, anti-nuclear analysts are opposed to invoking the nuclear option even if there is a rupture. In addition to emphasizing their continued confidence in the U.S. nuclear guarantee, they challenge the assumption that conflicts with China, Russia, and North Korea are inevitable. The growth in Chinese power-projection capabilities is not likely to disturb the military balance in East Asia for five to ten years, in this view, offering an opportunity to initiate discussion of conventional arms control and confidence-building measures before tensions develop. As for the Chinese nuclear threat, since China justifies its nuclear armament as a defensive response to U.S. and Russian nuclear deployments, especially in East Asia, Japan should pursue the redeployment and reduction of Chinese missiles as part of a broad nuclear arms control dialogue in East Asia, embracing the United States and Russia. By developing its own nuclear weapons, it is argued, Japan would only provoke a more belligerent posture on the part of both China and Russia.

The anti-nuclear argument relies heavily on the belief that intensified Sino-Japanese economic cooperation will reduce the danger of military conflict and should extend to cooperation in seabed petroleum development near the contested Senkaku (Tiao Yu Tai) islands and surrounding areas of the East China Sea. Similarly, just as pro-nuclear hawks are identified with a confrontational posture toward North Korea, so economic cooperation with Pyongyang is generally supported by anti-nuclear forces in the context of an overall normalization of relations.

While most opponents of nuclear weapons continue to posit indefinite reliance on the U.S. nuclear deterrent, Kumao Kaneko, a former director of the Nuclear Energy Division of the Foreign Ministry, has argued that "the continuation of the Security Treaty and the issue of the 'nuclear umbrella' should be viewed separately." Japan should continue to rely on the United States for protection in the event of a conventional attack, he writes, but should recognize that it is unrealistic to count on U.S. help in the event of a nuclear threat. "The United States would be highly unlikely to use its nuclear arms to defend Japan," Kaneko contends, "unless American forces in

Japan were exposed to extreme danger." It would be self-defeating for Japan to acquire nuclear weapons of its own, in his view, since this would lead North and South Korea, or a unified Korea, to follow suit, in addition to exacerbating tensions with Russia and China.

Kaneko's conclusion is that the most effective way for Japan to achieve nuclear security would be to pursue two related initiatives. Given the growing use of nuclear power in East Asia, Tokyo should take the lead in creating a regional atomic energy organization (ASIATOM) comparable to EURATOM ; and as this effort takes shape, it should promote negotiations on a Northeast Asia nuclear-free zone. The purpose of ASIATOM would be to facilitate transparency, the safe operation of nuclear facilities, the safe disposal of nuclear waste material, and, above all, the coordinated management of plutonium and enriched-uranium stocks held by all the member states, including Japan. Only when effective inspection and verification machinery is established under the ASIATOM treaty, Kaneko emphasizes, can the goal of a regional nuclear-free zone be realistically pursued.[47]

A NUCLEAR-FREE ZONE?

As an example of how a nuclear-free zone could be implemented, Kaneko proposes that such a zone encompass a circular area with a 2,000-kilometer radius from a central point at Panmunjon in Korea. Japan would invite North Korea, South Korea, Taiwan, and Mongolia to join in a treaty commitment not to make or acquire nuclear weapons or to permit them on their territory. Under a formula modeled after the nuclear-free zone treaty concluded by ten Southeast Asian nations in December 1995, China, Russia, and the United States would be asked to sign protocols affirming "respect" for the accord and pledging explicitly not to deploy or test nuclear weapons within the treaty zone and not to attack with nuclear weapons any of the five non-nuclear signatories.

Significantly, while the proposal would bar U.S. nuclear deployments inside the treaty zone, it would not affect U.S. missile-launching submarines and other U.S. nuclear deployments outside the area, thus leaving the United States free to use ICBMs against Asian countries other than the five signatories. Kaneko is one of numerous Japanese specialists who have made varying proposals for an ASIATOM organization and a Northeast Asia nuclear-free zone, but he is the only one who has formulated detailed model drafts of the implementing treaties.

27

Another significant initiative for a nuclear-free zone in Northeast Asia has been undertaken by John Endicott, former director of the Pentagon's National Institute of Strategic Studies, who has mobilized the support of prominent retired military officers from potential signatory countries for an institutionalized negotiating process designed to produce a treaty less ambitious in its scope than that proposed by Kaneko. A series of conferences has mapped specific plans to establish a Northeast Asia Limited Nuclear-Free Zone Agency charged with conducting negotiations leading to the projected treaty.

One of the key issues unresolved in the conferences so far is how to delimit the treaty zone. Endicott's own delimitation proposal would define a circular zone centered at Panmunjom with a radius of 1200 nautical miles embracing parts of China and Russia and all of Taiwan, Japan, Mongolia, and the two Koreas. The United States would pledge to respect the zone. The ultimate objective would be the prohibition of all nuclear deployments within this zone. Initially, however, only tactical nuclear weapons would be prohibited. Another proposal is for an elliptically shaped zone that would have its western border in northeast China and its eastern border in Alaska. Still another proposal for a North-Pacific Zone would bar nuclear deployments in specified areas within the signatory states.[48]

"POSSESSING THE 'WILL THAT WE CAN DO IT' IS IMPORTANT"

The changing international environment resulting from the end of the Cold War is only one of the factors that has rekindled the debate over nuclear policy in Japan. Just as the signing and ratification of the NPT became a focus of controversy until Japan decided on its final position in 1976, so the issue of whether to support the U.S. demand for the unconditional and indefinite extension of the treaty aroused intense discussion during the prelude to the 1995 NPT extension conference. In contrast with the bitter polarization between Right and Left that marked the pre-1976 debate, however, both the proponents and the opponents of nuclear weapons were united in their opposition to the American position in 1995.

The United States inadvertently forced the nuclear debate into the open in the course of its negotiations with Japan prior to the June 1993 Group of Seven (G-7) economic summit in Tokyo. At the 1992 Munich G-7 summit, Japan had joined with the United States in a statement "firmly" backing indefinite extension. In 1993, the United States sought Japanese support for a stronger statement backing unconditional as well as indefinite extension. The United States was seeking to head off moves by Third World countries seeking to condition extension of the treaty on a timebound commitment by the nuclear powers to phase out their own nuclear weapons in accordance with a key provision of the treaty, Article Six. This provision commits the nuclear powers to pursue "negotiations in good faith on effective measures relating to cessation of the arms race at an early date and to nuclear disarmament." To Washington's surprise, Japan refused to accept inclusion of the word "unconditional" in the 1993 summit communiqué and agreed only at the eleventh hour to join in reaffirming support for indefinite extension. Shortly after the Tokyo summit, Yoshifuni Okamoto, deputy director of the Foreign Ministry's Nuclear Division, underlined the Japanese belief that:

> The NPT is an unequal treaty. On the one hand, you have five countries that can have nuclear arms. On the other, all the others who are prohibited from having them. We have no intention of calling into question our commitment not to possess nuclear weapons. But if North Korea obtains nuclear weapons, there will be a debate in Japanese public opinion regarding the means of confronting this situation. And this could weaken our commitment to the NPT.[49]

Foreign Minister Muto made a similar statement on July 28, 1993, declaring that:

> If North Korea develops nuclear weapons and that becomes a threat to Japan, first there is the nuclear umbrella of the United States upon which we can rely. But if it comes down to a crunch, possessing the will that 'we can do it' is important.[50]

Muto added that Japan supported the indefinite extension of the NPT, prompting a rebuke by Prime Minister Kiichi Miyazawa, who said that the Foreign Minister's remarks were unauthorized.[51] Responding to the ensuing alarm in Washington, Miyazawa's successor, Morihiro Hosokawa, later declared his support in late August for indefinite extension. But Hosokawa immediately faced widespread opposition. "Even if agreement is reached to extend the treaty indefinitely," declared the *Asahi Shimbun*,

> Japan should take a firm stance to include a clause requiring the nuclear powers to abolish nuclear weapons within a limited period of time. Otherwise, indefinite extension would lead to making the privileged status of the nuclear powers an established matter. Is this really the right course for Japan—a country which suffered atomic bombing?[52]

The New York Times reported that the opponents of indefinite extension "have recently won many influential supporters in Japan." Some of these supporters, the *Times* said, are anti-nuclear leaders who believe that extension should be linked to nuclear disarmament, but "the real pressure" for opposing indefinite extension comes from "nationalists and rightists" who argue that Japan should keep its nuclear option open by seeking a limited extension. While overt support for nuclear weapons is limited, the *Times* added, government officials acknowledged that such support "has been expressed at confidential seminars by influential experts and politicians."[53]

Responding to public uneasiness over the NPT issue, the Japanese government introduced a little-noticed resolution in the United Nations on November 2, 1994, urging the nuclear weapon states "to further pursue negotiations on progressive and balanced reductions of nuclear weapons in the light of Article Six."[54] This provoked an angry encounter between the Japanese and U.S. Ambassadors to the Geneva Disarmament Conference, Yoshitomo Tanaka and Stephen Ledogar. Kept secret at the time, the incident surfaced in a *Washington Post* review of Japan's nuclear policy six months later:

> Japan's government had mixed feelings about its decision to back indefinite NPT extension in 1995, Tanaka said. Many Japanese politicians sincerely wanted the five nuclear powers, including the United States, to live up to their NPT pledge. The Japanese public was even more adamant; after all, they knew more than any people about the horrors of nuclear war.

> 'In a security arrangement such as the one the US and Japan have, certain things are expected,' Ledogar fumed, according to people familiar with the meeting . . . Nuclear partners, he continued, ought 'not to take steps, motivated by domestic politics, that are inconsistent with common security interests and arrangements.'[55]

The United States argued that passage of the resolution would strengthen opponents of indefinite extension. Japan countered that the non-proliferation cause would be strengthened if the nuclear powers demonstrated a recognition of their Article Six obligations. In the end, Japan attempted to appease the United States by removing the references to Article Six and negotiations in its draft. But the resolution did call upon the nuclear states in general terms "to pursue their efforts for nuclear disarmament with the ultimate objective of the elimination of nuclear weapons."[56] Even this indirect bow to Article Six led the United States to abstain when the resolution was adopted on November 16, 1995. Seven others, including Britain, France, North Korea, and Cuba, also abstained.

CLINTON'S HIROSHIMA 'BOMBSHELL'

The conflict between Tokyo and Washington at the United Nations received much less public attention in Japan than the acrimonious debate in the United States that in late 1994 and early 1995 accompanied the fiftieth anniversary of the Hiroshima and Nagasaki bombings. For months, Japanese newspapers on the Right and the Left alike closely followed each new development in the U.S. controversy over the Smithsonian Institution anniversary exhibit centering on the Enola Gay, the plane that dropped the first bomb. When the Smithsonian revamped its exhibit in the face of protests from conservatives, a leading Japanese TV commentator typified the outraged Japanese response with his objection that:

> The United States is trying to legitimize the atomic bomb. . . .
> The Enola Gay is presented here not as a warning against the great horror of nuclear war but as a holy relic, something above criticism, a national icon honoring the decision believed to be responsible for bringing World War II to an end.[57]

The angry mood generated by the Smithsonian controversy intensified when the U.S. Postal Service unveiled a proposed anniversary stamp depicting a mushroom cloud with the caption, "Atomic Bomb Hastens War's End." The subsequent withdrawal of the stamp resulting from President Bill Clinton's personal intervention did little to calm the waters in Japan because Clinton himself soon afterward took a surprisingly sharp and unequivocal stand justifying Harry Truman's decision to use nuclear weapons. A press conference questioner, Josette Shiner, Managing Editor of *The*

Washington Times, put the issue to the President in carefully neutral terms, observing that:

> Some have suggested that it's time to try to heal the wounds of World War II and that the United States should take the first step by apologizing for dropping the bomb on Hiroshima and Nagasaki. Should we apologize? And did Harry Truman make the right decision in dropping the bomb?

"No," answered the President. "And based on the facts he had before him, yes." [58] The profound impact of this blunt statement in Japan was heightened by the fact that it coincided with the publication of historical findings casting new doubt on whether the use of nuclear weapons was necessary to win the war.[59] Moreover, Clinton's stand was in marked contrast with the noncommittal responses given to similar questions by his predecessors. Presidents Carter, Kennedy, Johnson, Nixon, and Reagan all avoided direct replies.[60] Dwight D. Eisenhower categorically deplored the use of the bomb, stating that "it wasn't necessary to hit them with that awful thing."[61] George Bush was the only president prior to Clinton who categorically stated that "no apology is required. I was fighting out there, and American lives were saved by the bombings."[62]

Clinton no doubt made this statement with his domestic U.S. political audience in mind. But the effect in Japan[63] was to hand a potent new weapon to the advocates of a Japanese nuclear-weapons program. Memories of Hiroshima and Nagasaki are invoked not only by the opponents of nuclear weapons but by their proponents as well. The opponents believe that Japan's unique experience has given it a special responsibility to work for the elimination of nuclear weapons. The pro-nuclear minority, in contrast, seeks to exploit the sublimated feelings of humiliation and impotent rage resulting from this "victim" self-image. Only if Japan itself acquires nuclear weapons, they argue, will the nation be able to erase the traumatic impact of the bombings from the national psyche and stand up to the United States as an equal in economic disputes and global policy decision-making.

Significantly, one of the most impassioned opponents of the U.S.-Japan Security Treaty, former *Nihon Keizai* editor Yasuo Takeyama, is a survivor of Hiroshima. In a speech implying support for a nuclear weapons program, Takeyama declared:

> We Japanese have to admit very frankly with a sense of shame and regret that Japan has been a semi-independent nation

under the constraints of the Japan-U.S. Security Pact and Article 9 of the U.S.–imposed Constitution, which was forced upon Japan during the MacArthur occupation . . . We have to be courageous enough to restructure our post-war body politic: first, by amending or enacting a new constitution, and then by revising or rescinding the Security Pact . . . Even if Japan should eventually develop its own nuclear weapons, there would be no reason for Asian countries to fear Japan. The world has long learned to live with a nuclear-armed United States, Russia, France, Britain, China and perhaps even North Korea. There is no reason to suspect that Japan's adoption of nuclear weapons would be anything more than a policy of defense and deterrence following the principle of Mutual Assured Destruction.[64]

Former Prime Minister Kiichi Miyazawa, who had warned in 1971 that latent pro-nuclear sentiment could explode if "the major nations . . . push Japan around too much," has expressed similar anxieties during the post–Cold War debate over national security policy. These anxieties underlie his opposition to New Frontier Party leader Ichiro Ozawa's view that Japan should become a "normal country." Ozawa's plan to send armed Japanese combat forces abroad on U.N. peacekeeping missions would open a Pandora's Box, Miyazawa has suggested, since:

Looking ahead, if that leads to revising the Constitution and Japan has armed forces, before long the argument would definitely emerge that having nuclear weapons would be the most economical form of defense. Since conscription would be all but impossible in Japan, it would be necessary to rely on volunteers, but then the personnel costs would be quite high. Nuclear weapons armament would be much more economical, they would say. If there were problems about locating nuclear missiles on land, then pretty soon they would insist that Japan could deploy them on submarines.[65]

WILL JAPAN GO NUCLEAR?

What factors could eradicate Japan's "nuclear allergy" and lead to a new consensus in favor of developing nuclear weapons?

Professor Fuji Kamiya of the National Defense Academy, one of Japan's most respected security specialists, emphasizes three factors, in this order of importance:

- A failure of the five nuclear powers to move toward the reduction and eventual elimination of their nuclear weapons;

- The perception of an emerging military threat to Japan from Russia, China, or North Korea; and

- A Japanese loss of confidence in the U.S. nuclear umbrella as an effective deterrent to Russian, Chinese, and North Korean military pressures.[66]

This assessment is supported by the preceding analysis of the Japanese debate on nuclear policy during the past three decades. Many analysts focus narrowly on threat perceptions and the credibility of the U.S. deterrent. But Kamiya has reflected the character of the debate more accurately by placing nuclear arms reductions at the top of his list. From the start, as we have seen, many Japanese on both the Right and the Left have been deeply disturbed by the built-in inequities in the NPT and the prospect of a static global hierarchy in which five privileged powers, excluding Japan, would permanently hold a dominant position. While these doubts were submerged during the Cold War, they burst to the surface in a series of conflicts between Japan and the United States over the terms for the extension of the NPT in 1995. The American "victory" in these conflicts was purchased at the cost of a sublimated resentment that could erupt unpredictably unless the nuclear powers take steps to honor Article Six.

Whether or not there is progress in global nuclear arms control, increased military tensions with Russia, China, or North Korea could tip the scales in the Japanese debate. As Kamiya observes, Japan would not necessarily go nuclear in response to such tensions if the U.S.–Japan relationship is stable and the U.S. nuclear deterrent remains credible. But U.S.–Japan relations are likely to be increasingly troubled in both the security and economic spheres. Japanese sentiment for a greatly reduced American military presence is growing despite the concessions made by President Clinton in his 1996 summit meeting with Prime Minister Ryutaro Hashimoto. The United States wants much more Japanese defense cooperation and "burden-sharing" than the Japanese public is ready to accept. Trade disputes are intensifying. During the Cold War, the United States often pulled its punches in economic disputes in order to avoid the risk of a rupture in the alliance. Now pressures are building up for a more determined U.S. posture in economic disputes. To say, as American officials do, that "we have insulated our security ties from trade frictions" is whistling in the dark. Tensions in the Japanese-American relationship are likely to persist during the decades ahead, eroding Japanese confidence in the credibility of the U.S. deterrent regardless of the formal U.S. declaratory posture.

U.S. POLICY AND JAPAN'S NUCLEAR FUTURE: FOUR KEY ISSUES

In such a fluid environment, the policy choices made by the United States on four critical arms control and non-proliferation issues could well have a determining impact on whether Japan decides to go nuclear. Continued American adherence to the Japan–U.S. Security Treaty, in and of itself, would not necessarily assure a non-nuclear Japan in the absence of a new American approach to these issues.

Reductions in Nuclear Weaponry. The U.S.–Japan Study Group on Arms Control and Non-Proliferation, co-sponsored by the Carnegie Endowment and International House of Japan, has recommended that the United States and Russia consider "progressive and balanced reductions of their strategic weapons to 300 to 500 each" in a series of negotiations beginning with START III. This dialogue would be accompanied by broader five-power negotiations that would seek to stabilize Chinese, British, and French arsenals while the U.S.–Russian build-down proceeds and would map long-term steps to move toward zero in parallel with non-proliferation efforts.[67] Meaningful action by the nuclear powers to implement these recommendations with timebound commitments would greatly strengthen the opponents of nuclear weapons in Japan. First, such steps would ease the festering resentment toward the NPT as an unequal treaty. Furthermore, they would open up the possibility of Chinese participation in regional arms control discussions, in which Chinese medium-range missile deployments could be addressed.

The most telling strategic argument made by the pro-nuclear forces is that China's DF-3 missile deployments pose a direct threat to Japan. China maintains that its nuclear weapons are a defensive response to American and Russian deployments in Northeast Asia. As a precondition for taking part in regional arms control discussions, Beijing calls for reductions in American and Russian nuclear deployments so that China will not be negotiating from a position of inferiority. For this reason, as Gerald Segal of the International

35

Institute of Strategic Studies observes, "from the point of view of Northeast Asia, it is important that further reductions in Russian and American arsenals include, if not feature, reductions in weapons deployed in Northeast Asia."[68]

In addition to seeking reductions in U.S. and Russian nuclear forces as a precondition for joining in a regional dialogue, China has made clear that the United States and Russia would also have to participate and discuss further trade-offs. At present, while urging East Asian powers to establish regional forums for the discussion of security issues, the United States has balked at suggestions that its own deployments should be on the table in regional arms control negotiations. Russia has made repeated proposals to the United States for mutual force reductions in the Pacific since 1987.

Redefining the Nuclear Umbrella. China, emphasizing its long-standing pledge not to use nuclear weapons first, points to the U.S. and Russian refusal to emulate this No-First-Use policy as a justification for its nuclear-weapons deployments. Thus, a shift in the U.S. and Russian position on this issue would be necessary to facilitate regional arms control and denuclearization initiatives.

At present, the phrase "nuclear umbrella" is used loosely to describe protection against both a nuclear and a conventional attack. James Leonard, former U.S. representative at the Geneva Disarmament Conference, has offered a useful distinction, calling protection against a nuclear attack alone "Umbrella A" and protection extended also against a conventional attack "Umbrella B."[69] During the Cold War, American strategy explicitly included "Umbrella B" protection. The doctrine of "flexible response" envisaged the possible use of nuclear weapons first in western Europe, where NATO faced massive Soviet conventional forces. In the case of East Asia, American readiness to use nuclear weapons first was implicit in the deployment of nuclear weaponry in the Seventh Fleet and in South Korea.

Despite the withdrawal of U.S. tactical nuclear weapons from forward deployment in East Asia, the option of first use remains open, since the United States has not ruled out their redeployment in the event of a crisis. Yet even in Europe, the formal NATO doctrine now is that nuclear weapons would only be used as a "last resort." Moreover, as Leonard points out, "with the cold war over, there is a clear trend toward universalizing No First Use," since the pledges ('negative security assurances') increasingly being given by nuclear-weapon states not to use nuclear weapons against non-nuclear signatories of the NPT "mean, in effect, the end of Umbrella B . . . We will soon have a de facto universal No First Use policy in place, despite its formal rejection by the three Western nuclear powers and the recent fluctuations in Russia's posture."[70]

A Regional Nuclear Safeguards Regime. The concept of an ASIATOM counterpart to EURATOM discussed earlier is being promoted in Japan by those who support nuclear power for civilian purposes. As elaborated by Kumao Kaneko and others, this concept envisages the creation of an effective system for monitoring the nuclear-material stockpiles of member states, including Japan, an aspect of the proposal that is being quietly resisted by Japanese pronuclear forces.

The establishment of an ASIATOM would be the most effective way to reduce suspicions of Japan's intentions on the part of China, North and South Korea, and Taiwan—if it included effective monitoring machinery that would prevent the diversion of nuclear material for military purposes.

Many observers argue that monitoring is not enough and that suspicions would persist in the absence of the multilateral control of fissile material stockpiles and interdependent regional nuclear fuel cycle arrangements that would make it technically impossible for individual countries to pursue nuclear weapons development. But even regional monitoring machinery would be difficult to achieve, as a practical matter, and would be an important step in the right direction.

Opponents of the civilian use of plutonium in Japan and elsewhere object that creation of an ASIATOM would legitimize the use of plutonium. But the advantages of such a system in improving the East Asian security climate would outweigh these concerns. A regional approach to nuclear-energy cooperation would not be restricted to plutonium-based programs and would not preclude continued efforts in Japan to downgrade the plutonium program, such as the campaign touched off by the Monju accident.

The United States has been cool to the ASIATOM concept, fearful that it would nullify many aspects of its bilateral nuclear cooperation agreements with member states and thus end U.S. leverage over their nuclear programs. In the case of Japan, however, the extent of U.S. leverage has steadily diminished, and the collective leverage exercised by other ASIATOM members on Japan might well prove to be more potent than that of the United States.

A Northeast Asia Nuclear-Free Zone. The pro-nuclear forces in Japan would be greatly weakened if the United States modified its current policies by pursuing nuclear disarmament, redefining the nuclear umbrella, and supporting a regional nuclear-safeguards regime. But the best form of insurance against a nuclear-armed Japan would be a regional nuclear-free zone agreement similar to the 1995 Southeast Asian treaty. Such an agreement would reinforce nuclear disarmament and would logically accompany the establishment of an ASIATOM organization. The machinery created by ASIATOM to monitor the nuclear programs of member states could be broadened to verify whether signatories of the nuclear-free zone agreement are keeping their pledge not to develop nuclear weapons.

By its nature, a nuclear-free zone agreement would obviate the need for a pledge of U.S. nuclear protection. The United States would agree not to use or deploy nuclear weapons in the zone, or to threaten their use, if the other nuclear powers made the same commitment. In the event of the use or threat of use of nuclear weapons by another nuclear weapon state that is a party to the treaty, the United States could redeploy nuclear weapons in the region.

The Southeast Asian treaty commits the signatories not to "develop, manufacture or otherwise acquire, station or transport nuclear weapons by any means, or test and use nuclear weapons" either inside or outside the zone and commits them to prohibit other states from violating these restrictions within their territory. But implementation of the treaty has been blocked by the refusal of the nuclear powers to sign a protocol to the treaty pledging to respect its provisions. The United States, in particular, wants assurances that the treaty would not impede the transit of its nuclear-armed ships and submarines.

Although the treaty permits the "innocent passage" of warships and submarines, the overflight of aircraft, and stopovers in ports and airfields, it gives each signatory state the right to decide whether passage in a given case is indeed "innocent" or is related to the possible use of nuclear weapons in combat operations.

Welcoming the treaty, the Japanese daily *Mainichi* said that it "raises the issue of a possible similar agreement for Northeast Asia" and called for "resilient efforts to create a chain of nuclear-free zones by nations that reject the possession of nuclear weapons of their own, denounce the use of such weapons by others and refuse the protection offered by nuclear umbrellas."[71]

This endorsement of the nuclear-free zone concept by a leading mainstream newspaper reflects an increasing readiness in Japan to question the premises of the U.S.–Japan security relationship. For example, former Prime Minister Morihiro Hosokawa asked in March 1996:

> How do we reconcile our dependence on the US nuclear umbrella with our purported commitment to an anti-nuclear policy? Why are 47,000 troops necessary in Japan? How much will Japan be involved in the global role of US forces based in our country?
>
> The Security Treaty provides only for the defense of Japan and the 'peace and security' of the Far East. But in reality, the US forces stationed in Japan are designed to play a leading military role as far away as the Middle East. Japan continues to give uncritical support to US strategy and has not seriously discussed the level of forces deployed on Japanese territory, or even the need for them, with the United States.[72]

Nevertheless, despite a growing mood of reappraisal, the prospects for a nuclear-free zone in Northeast Asia appear dim in the foreseeable future against the larger backdrop of regional developments. In particular, continuing tension between North and South Korea is likely to block the new U.S. policy initiatives that would be necessary to pave the way for the participation of the two Koreas in a nuclear-free zone.

The United States is not likely to withdraw its nuclear umbrella over South Korea, or even to rule out the first use of nuclear weapons in Korea, until this tension begins to subside. Such initiatives would be bitterly resisted by the South until Pyongyang permits the full range of nuclear inspections needed to assess its nuclear capabilities. American and Japanese policy in Korea therefore should be directed to creating an environment favorable to the final resolution of the nuclear issue in Pyongyang. The prospects for North Korean agreement to the comprehensive inspection of its nuclear program would be greatly enhanced by American and Japanese economic cooperation and political normalization with Pyongyang and by the replacement of the 1953 Korean Armistice with a more stable peacekeeping system suited to post–Cold War realignments.

THE FUTURE OF NUCLEAR WEAPONS

In the absence of a regional environment favorable to the establishment of a nuclear-free zone, the Japanese nuclear-policy debate will focus increasingly on the outcome of the global struggle now in progress over the future of nuclear weapons. Japan's nuclear future will be influenced in part by the domestic controversy in Japan itself over the safety of a plutonium-based nuclear program resulting from the Monju reactor accident. But what Japan decides will depend primarily on whether the United States and Russia make the reductions in their nuclear arsenals necessary to draw China and the other nuclear powers into a continuing process of nuclear disarmament.

In a world moving toward denuclearization, however gradually, Japan's anti-nuclear consensus is likely to hold firm. In a world with a frozen power structure dominated by five countries claiming the right to a perpetual nuclear monopoly, Japanese nationalism is likely to triumph, in the end, over the "nuclear allergy."

NOTES

[1]*Mugunghwa Kk'Och'i P'iossumnida* (The Rose of Sharon Has Blossomed), Seoul: Haenaem Publishing Company, 1994, sold 1.3 million sets of the complete trilogy and 4.1 million copies of separate volumes. Sales for a successful book in South Korea rarely exceed 300,000.

[2]Selig S. Harrison, "North Korea and Nuclear Weapons: South Korean Responses," a paper prepared for a conference on "The Regional Implications of Korean Proliferation" sponsored by the Science Applications International Corporation, May 19, 1992, esp. pp. 5–6. See also "Seoul Planned Nuclear Weapons Until 1991," *Jane's Defense Weekly*, April 2, 1994, p. 1.

[3]September, 1977, p. 76.

[4]*Haek Mulli Hakja Lee Hwi So* (Nuclear Physicist Lee Hwi So), a biography by Kong Suk Ha, a professor at Doksong Women's College, published by Puri Publishing Co., Seoul, appeared in 1989. The same author's novel, *Lee Hwi So Sosol* (Lee Hwi So the Novel), also published by Puri Publishing Co., appeared in 1993. Neither work contained factual evidence linking Lee to Park's program. However, Kong stated that he had interviewed Park's family and Lee's family in preparing his novel. The novel depicts Lee as helping the nuclear program, and the biography contains a photo of a National Service Medal posthumously awarded to Lee by Park praising his "contributions to Korean scientific achievement."

[5]Press Conference, Foreign Ministry, Tokyo, February 17, 1966.

[6]"Nuclear Arms and Opposition," *Japan Times Weekly*, January 27, 1968, p. 4.

[7]"Nuclear Armament Possible But Unrealistic: Secret Reports," *Asahi*, November 13, 1994, p.1.

[8]Charles J. Hanley, Associated Press dispatch from Tokyo, May 4, 1995.

[9]"Nuclearization Possible Technically," *Mainichi*, July 12, 1968.

[10]"Armed With Nuclear Weapons in Future: Former Prime Minister Gives Lecture on Security Problems," *Nihon Keizai*, March 15, 1969.

[11]"The Capability to Develop Nuclear Weapons Should be Kept: Ministry of Foreign Affairs Secret Document in 1969," *Mainichi*, August 1, 1994, p. 1.

[12]Arjun Makhijani of the Institute for Energy and Environmental Research obtained a translation of pp. 62–68 of the study from a member of the Japanese Diet with Foreign Ministry contacts. This translation contains all of the passages reported in *Mainichi*. However, subsection 9 on p. 67 also includes the two sentences cited, which are not reported in *Mainichi*.

[13]American Embassy briefing, Tokyo, October 8, 1969.

[14]"Agreed Minute to Joint Communiqué of United States President Nixon and Japanese Prime Minister Sato Issued on November 21, 1969," (Top Secret), Washington, two pages. See Kei Wakaizumi, *Tasaku Nakarishi o Shinzemu to Hossu* (I want to Believe There was No Other Alternative), Tokyo: Bungeishunju Limited, 1994.

[15]This is based on a tape recording of Sato's comments to business executives at Keidanren headquarters in Tokyo on December 8, 1969, translated for me by Seiji Yamaoka of *The Washington Post*. See Selig S. Harrison, "Japanese Wary of Nuclear Treaty," *Washington Post*, December 15, 1969, p. 3.

[16]"Statement of the Government of Japan On the Occasion of the Signing of the Treaty on the Non-Proliferation of Nuclear Weapons," February 3, 1970, esp. pp. 2, 5, and 6.

[17]Selig S. Harrison, "Japan's Defense Minister Drops Advocacy of a Nuclear Force," *The Washington Post*, March 5, 1970, p. 3.

[18]Yasuhiro Nakasone, "The International Environment and the Defense of Japan in the 1970's," an address delivered at the Harvard Club of Japan, June 30, 1970, p. 8.

[19]Selig S. Harrison, "Japan To Be 'Medium-Rank' Power," *International Herald Tribune*, October 21, 1970, p. 1. See also "Gist of White Paper on Defense," *Japan Times*, October 1970, p. 20.

[20]His formal title was Acting Chairman. The honorific chairmanship is held concurrently by the Minister of State for Science and Technology, a political appointee. Arisawa served under a succession of seven ministers.

[21]"Ningen No Chie Nante Asahaka Na Manodesu" (Humanity's Wisdom Is a Shallow Thing), *Asahi*, September 12, 1972. Arisawa's revelation was recalled by a columnist on the occasion of his death, "Kyo No Mondai" (Topic of the Day). *Asahi*, March 8, 1988, p. 55.

[22]Lowell Ponte, "Nippon Goes Nuclear," *The Progressive*, September, 1973, p. 32.

[23]*Asahi*, October 15, 1980, p. 8.

[24]Address to the Carnegie Endowment Study Group on Japan's Role In Non-Proliferation and Arms Control, Washington, March 1, 1994.

[25]"Miyazawa on Nuclearism," *Far Eastern Economic Review*, December 18, 1971, pp. 21–22.

[26]*Defense Report*, Statement of Secretary of Defense Melvin R. Laird before the Senate Armed Services Committee on the FY 1972–76 Defense Program and the 1972 Defense Budget, 92nd Congress, 1st session, March 15, 1971, pp. 15, 75–77.

[27]Ibid., p. 22.

[28]For the authorized text of Friedheim's briefing, see Department of State, Unclassified Tokyo dispatch 6709, July 7,1971, addressed to the Secretary of Defense and signed by Friedheim. The SABMIS comment has been excised from this text but is recorded in my notes and those of others present.

[29]Yasuo Takeyama, "Bei No Shinsekai Senryaku to Nihon-II" (The New U.S. World Strategy and Japan-Part II), *Nihon Keizai*, November 30, 1971, p. 1. See also "Japanese-American Bilateral Meeting," transcript of the Third Annual Japan–U.S. Conference, International Press Institute, San Diego, November 26–29, 1972, p. 76.

[30]*Time*, January 3, 1972, p. 11.

[31]Article I, Implementing Agreement of *The Agreement Between the United States and Japan Concerning Peaceful Uses of Atomic Energy*, H. Doc. 128, 100th Congress, 1st Session, 8 (November 9, 1987).

[32]The author is indebted to Christopher Paine and Victor Gilinsky for expert guidance on technical issues related to the Japanese nuclear program.

[33]Jinzaburo Takagi, Director of the Citizens Nuclear Information Center of Japan, made the estimate of 10 kilograms in a memorandum to me dated March 22, 1996. Greenpeace International, citing British nuclear physicist Frank Barnaby, estimates that "as much as 70 kilograms" could accumulate in the blanket each year if the net annual production of the reactor reaches its full potential of 144 kilograms. *The Unlawful Plutonium Alliance: Japan's Supergrade Plutonium and The Role of the United States*, Greenpeace International, Amsterdam: September, 1994, p. 10.

[34]Jinzaburo Takagi states in a memorandum dated March 22, 1996, that the Joyo accumulation in the radial blanket was officially reported to have been 22 kilograms. He estimates that there are an additional 18 kilograms in the axial blanket. The blankets are now in storage.

[35]Victor Gilinsky, "Fast Breeder Reactors and the Spread of Plutonium," Memorandum RM-5148-PR, March 1967, Santa Monica, California: The RAND Corporation, pp. vii, 28.

[36]Op cit., *The Unlawful Plutonium Alliance.*

[37]Tom Clancy, *Debt of Honor,* New York: G. P. Putnam's Sons, 1994, esp. pp. 205–18.

[38]The author is indebted to John Pike, Director of the Space Policy Project of the Federation of American Scientists, for assistance in developing this estimate and for other expert guidance on technical issues related to the Japanese space program.

[39]*Over the Pacific: Japanese Space Policy Into the Twenty-First Century,* Dubuque, Iowa: Kendall-Hunt Publishing Company, 1992.

[40]Ibid., p. 125–26.

[41]Ibid., p. 45.

[42]Ibid., p. 127.

[43]Conversation with the author, February 12, 1996.

[44]Kyodo News Service, Tokyo, June 17, 1994.

[45]Kobayashi Yosaji, ed., *1970: An Approach to Revisions of the Security Treaty,* Tokyo: Yomiuri Shimbun, 1966, Part II, Chapter 2, pp. 109–110.

[46]Sam Jameson, "A Reluctant Superpower Agonizes Over Military," *Los Angeles Times,* August 1, 1995, p. 1.

[47]Kumao Kaneko, "Japan Needs No Umbrella," *The Bulletin of the Atomic Scientists,* March/April, 1996, pp. 46–51. For other Japanese proposals relating to the ASIATOM concept, see "Experts Call for Asian Nuclear Pact," *Nikkei Weekly,* February 20, 1995, p. 4.

[48]Details of the Endicott effort can be found in the report of a conference sponsored by the Center for International Strategy, Technology and Policy, University of Georgia, *Toward a Limited Nuclear Free Zone in Northeast Asia: Senior Panel's Deliberations on a Draft Initial Agreement,* Atlanta: February 24, 1995. The signatories of this statement were General Kim Jaechang, former Vice-Chairman of the Joint Chief of Staff, Republic of Korea Army; Lt. General Toshiyuki Shikata, former Commander of the Northern Army, Japan Ground Self-Defense Force; Major General V. N. Bunin, former Director of Far Eastern Affairs, Russian General Staff, and Professor Xuetong Yan, Deputy Director, China Institute of Contemporary International Relations.

[49]Interview with the French daily *Liberation,* July 9, 1993, cited in FBIS-EAS-93-2, July 13, 1993, p. 1.

[50]Sam Jameson, "Foreign Minister Says Japan Will Need Nuclear Arms if North Korea Threatens," *Los Angeles Times,* July 29, 1993, p. 3.

[51]"Muto's Remarks Made Without Permission," Kyodo dispatch cited in FBIS-EAS-93-144, July 29, 1993, p. 4.

[52]"Go Slowly on Extension of Non-Proliferation Treaty," *Asahi Evening News,* August 30, 1993, p. 10.

[53]James Sterngold, "Japan Rethinking Nuclear Pact," *The New York Times,* August 7, 1993, p. 6.

[54]United Nations, General Assembly, Japan: Draft Resolution, *Nuclear Disarmament With a View to the Ultimate Elimination of Nuclear Weapons,* A/C 1 49/L. 33, November 2, 1994, First Committee.

[55]"Rethinking the Bomb," Part 6, 'A Hard Sell for Treaty Renewal,' *The Washington Post,* April 14, 1995, p. A27.

[56]United Nations, General Assembly, Japan: Revised Draft Resolution, *Nuclear Disarmament With a View to the Ultimate Elimination of Nuclear Weapons,* A/O 1/49/L.55/ Rev. 1, November 16, 1994.

[57]T. R. Reid, "Japanese Media Decry Enola Gay Exhibition," *The Washington Post,* June 29, 1995, p. 4.

[58]April 7, 1995, Dallas, at the convention of the American Society of Newspaper Editors.

[59]For example, see Gar Alperovitz, *The Decision to Use the Atomic Bomb,* New York: Alfred A. Knopf, 1995.

[60]The John F. Kennedy Library and the Lyndon B. Johnson Library state that neither Kennedy nor Johnson made direct references to U.S. use of the atomic bomb. Carter visited Hiroshima on May 25, 1984, but stated only that "the lesson of Hiroshima shall not be forgotten, and all of us will continue to seek ways to avert mass genocide by nuclear weapons." Nixon (July 29, 1985) and Reagan (August 6, 1985), asked directly for comment on whether the bomb should have been used, made non-committal replies.

[61]Cited in Colman McCarthy, "Since Hiroshima: Forty Years of Insanity and Dumb Luck," *The Washington Post,* August 4, 1985, Style section, p. 1.

[62]"No Apology Necessary," *Time,* December 16, 1991, p. 53.

[63]For example, see T. R. Reid, "Clinton Comment Stirs Demands for A-Bomb Apology, *The Washington Post,* April 14, 1995, p. 24, and "Willis Witter, "Clinton's Words Revive Japan's Ire Over A-Bombs," *The Washington Times,* April 18, 1995, p. A11.

[64]Yasuo Takeyama, "Japan and its Role in Asia," an address at the 1992 Taipei YPO World Conference, April 27–May 1, 1992, pp. 15–16 and 19.

[65]"Nichibei Kankei 'Taitoo Na Kankei' to iu Ukareta Hanashi de Wa Nai" (Is 'A Normal Country' the Path Toward Nuclear Armament?), Interview With Former Prime Minister Miyazawa, *AERA,* published weekly by the *Asahi Shimbun,* March 21, 1994, pp. 18–19.

[66]Cited in Bunraku Yoshino, "Japan and Energy Security," an address to the Energy Security Group sponsored by the Council on Foreign Relations and the Japan Atomic Industrial Forum, Washington, March 14, 1995. p. 20.

[67] *The United States, Japan and the Future of Nuclear Weapons,* Report of the U.S–Japan Study Group on Arms Control and Non-Proliferation After the Cold War, co-sponsored by the Carnegie Endowment for International Peace and International House of Japan, Washington, 1995, esp. pp. 5–22.

[68]"What Can We Do About Nuclear Forces in Northeast Asia?," The Korean Journal of Defense Analysis, January 1995, p. 49.

[69]"Nuclear Umbrellas," in *Nuclear Policies in Northeast Asia,* ed. Andrew Mack, United Nations Institute for Disarmament Research, Geneva, 1995, pp. 43–47.

[70]Ibid.

[71]December 18, 1995.

[72]Address to Council on Foreign Relations, March 11, 1996. Washington.

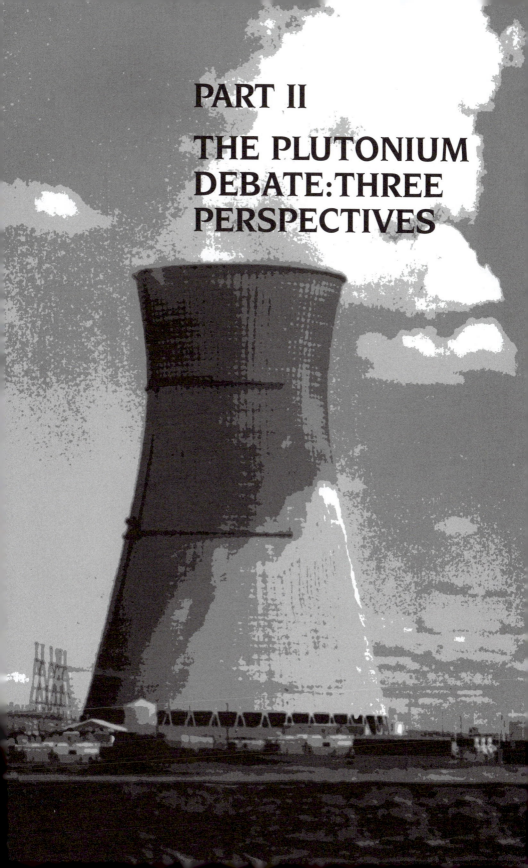

PART II

THE PLUTONIUM DEBATE: THREE PERSPECTIVES

CHAPTER 1

WHY PLUTONIUM IS A 'MUST' FOR JAPAN

ATSUYUKI SUZUKI

THE HISTORICAL CONTEXT

Why is it that Japan has promoted and will promote the peaceful uses of plutonium? The reliance on plutonium in the Japanese nuclear-power program has attracted international attention and controversy. Against this background, it would be useful to go back to the starting point in the development of nuclear energy in order to take a historical look at problems associated with the peaceful uses of nuclear material and thereby find guidance in our efforts to determine the best course for the future.

From the beginning of the time when Japan, like some other countries, was planning to use nuclear energy for peaceful purposes, notably for purposes of power generation, the use of plutonium as fuel has been a matter for consideration. The United States was the first nation to start research and development on the peaceful uses of nuclear energy. The first experimental reactor ever built in the United States was "Clementine," a fast reactor, which reached the initial chain reaction of nuclear fission in 1946 at Los Alamos Scientific Laboratory.[1]

Initially, using fast reactors for nuclear power was the prevailing idea in nuclear technology, because it is difficult to achieve a nuclear chain reaction using natural uranium and, as such, it is hard to make effective fuel in this manner. From a purely technical point of view, the prevailing idea was that a more efficient use for uranium could be found if, in a fast reactor, it could be made into plutonium for use as fuel. So it was not unreasonable at all to find a use for plutonium. People thinking about utilizing nuclear energy(specif-ically about changing uranium resources into energy for use as elec-tricity(sought, from a technical point of view, to use a reactor for converting uranium into plutonium, from which energy could be extracted if it was fissioned. This was the starting point in the devel-opment of nuclear energy.

While the above was the prevailing idea in nuclear technology, the United States was developing technologies for uranium enrich-ment and nuclear ships. A nuclear ship is not an electric-power-gen-erating unit but uses heat from a nuclear reactor as its power source. For this purpose, the Americans developed a light-water reactor (LWR) using enriched uranium, as it was more liable to fission. Then they began to consider using a similar reactor for nuclear power, thinking this might be a more practical way to find a use for nuclear energy.

This led to the development of an LWR power plant. Nevertheless, there was still a preference for fast reactors from the standpoint of resource economy. The idea persisted that plutonium was the fuel of choice.

In the 1970s, however, oil price shocks brought about a dras-tic change in the world energy situation. In contrast with the "gold-en 60s," as the decade was called in the United States, Americans saw an ominous shadow looming in the 1970s. The U.S. economy ceased to grow as fast as it had in the preceding decade. Consequently, the demand for electricity slowed down. The cir-cumstances were such that the United States had less incentive for the development of fast reactors. It was in this context that American projects for the civilian utilization of plutonium fell through.[2]

Japanese industry, in contrast, was tenacious enough to recov-er from the heavy damage brought about by the oil price shocks of the 1970s and managed to show considerable growth in the 1980s. In terms of per capita gross national product, for instance, Japan surpassed the United States. The demand for electricity in Japan basically continued to increase. Japan, however, is not blessed with indigenous uranium resources. Therefore, with energy security in mind, high hopes were held out that plutonium would present the nation with a technology-intensive resource.

In addition, in contrast with the short-range approach of their American counterparts, the Japanese utility companies were pre-pared to base their plans on long-range supply and demand projections. Since a long-range program was what the Japanese inevitably had to carry out, it followed that the development of fast reactors was a matter of great importance. Actually, as is shown in table 1-1, the Long-Term Programs for the Development and Utilization of Nuclear Energy in Japan—recommended every five years by the Japanese Atomic Energy Commission—have continuously promoted the technological development of fast reactors and fuel reprocessing.

1-1. Long-Term Programs for the Development and Utilization of Nuclear Energy in Japan, by Year

1956	—Zero-power FBR program —Secured uranium supply system —Basic research on reprocessing
1961	—LWR introduction —Enriched uranium import —Recycling technology R&D
1967	—Safety assurance —Enrichment technology R&D —Advanced reactor R&D (PNC)
1972	—Site promotion —FBR and ATR programs —Commercial reprocessing program
1978	—LWR technology improvement —Fuel-cycle industry development —Monju project promotion
1982	—Plutonium recycling program —Technology transfer to private sector —Commercial enrichment program
1987	—Commercialization of R&D results —MOX fuel-fabrication program —Stimulation of fundamental research

PNC = Power Reactor and Nuclear Fuel Development Corporation
FBR = fast-breeder reactor
ATR = advanced thermal reactor
MOX = plutonium-and-uranium mixed oxide
LWR = light-water reactor

THE CASE FOR RECYCLING NUCLEAR FUEL

I t should be noted that the Japanese nuclear authorities require that nuclear power plants, whenever faced with the unloading of spent fuel and the loading of new fuel, must make a prior decision as to what to do with the fuel after it has been burnt. So the electric utilities are definitely obligated sooner or later to reprocess the spent fuels that their plants discharge. The reprocessing of spent fuels for the purpose of plutonium recycling is a requirement that must be met under Japan's national nuclear-power development program.

I have been arguing for some time that it would be too much of a fixed, entrenched idea to insist that spent fuel should be reprocessed and recycled as soon as possible.[3] There is no doubt about the wisdom of reprocessing and recycling, but questions remain as to how much of the spent fuel should be reprocessed and recycled and how fast. The trend of the long-term world market for uranium, the trend of nuclear-power development in Japan, and the international situation will have to be taken into account in considering these questions. Such a calculus may lead to the creation of spent fuels that cannot be reprocessed for a while, and the best way to cope with them will be to keep them in safe and planned stockpiles.

In any case, Japan doubts the wisdom of disposing of spent fuels as waste. For a country that is small in land space, prone to frequent earthquakes, endowed with rivers and streams, encircled by the sea, and confronted with many other natural constraints, it would be no easy task to dispose of spent fuels as waste. The disposal of spent fuel as it is might be one choice for a country like the United States, which has large expanses of land, including uninhabited desert areas. But what about Japan? I think it is a big question.

Japan has to buy its uranium from other countries. There are environmental problems of varying severity in countries that mine for uranium. The exploitation of natural resources other than uranium may raise such problems. Environmental problems in other countries are not to be resolved by Japan, but they are something to be taken into consideration. I would say that concern about environmental factors must have priority for Asians, or at any rate for the Japanese, considering their particular feelings about friendship and cohabitation. Since it is important that resources be recycled to ensure their conservation and environmental protection on a global scale, I believe that it is necessary to put an emphasis on the Oriental spirit of consideration, on the importance of seeing things in a long-range perspective.

Japan is now one of the most advanced nuclear-power countries; nuclear-power reactors and oil-fired plants are the largest sources of energy for the generation of electricity. Nearly 30 percent of all electricity is now provided by more than forty-five nuclear-power plants, totaling approximately 40,000 megawatts of electrical generating capacity.

The number of additional reactors being planned is limited, mainly because of the difficulty of procuring new sites. However, more plants are under construction that will bring the total capacity to about 45,000 megawatts by the year 2000. To meet both future demand for electricity, which is projected to increase continuously albeit moderately, and the requirements for protecting the global environment, Japanese electric utilities will have to rely more upon nuclear power. It is anticipated that plans to build some additional plants will be made in the near future.

With nuclear power contributing to Japan's overall energy supply system as a major source of electrical power, the nuclear-fuel-cycle sector is expanding correspondingly. In particular, the projects to construct fuel-cycle facilities at Rokkashomura will form the core of Japan's nuclear-fuel-cycle sector.

The biggest facility at the Rokkashomura center is the reprocessing plant, now under construction, which will enter the hot-operation phase shortly after the year 2000. The maximum annual capacity of the plant will be 800 tons of nuclear spent fuels reprocessed, and it is now expected to reach its full-scale operation around the year 2005. When reprocessing 800 tons of LWR spent fuel, 4.5 to 5 tons of fissile plutonium can usually be recovered, which is equivalent to 6 or 7 tons of total plutonium. (In most cases, about 70 percent of total plutonium is fissile.) By using those amounts of plutonium, roughly 100 tons of plutonium-and-uranium mixed oxide (MOX) fuel can potentially be produced for use at LWRs.

After the year 2005, Japan's total annual demand for LWR fuel will be more than 1,000 tons, indicating that the potential maximum capacity of the Rokkashomura plant will meet less than 10 percent of the nationwide total demand. This seems quite reasonable in the sense that Japan's intended plan for making use of recycled plutonium is to prepare the social and technological infrastructure that it requires on a minimum industrial scale. The yearly plutonium balance we can expect under the current situation is shown in table 1-2.[4]

There are three sources of Japanese plutonium: the Tokai reprocessing plant, the Rokkashomura reprocessing plant, and the overseas reprocessing services contracted.

The Power Reactor and Nuclear Fuel Development Corporation (PNC) has a plant producing an annual average of 0.4 tons of fissile plutonium at Tokai. The production from the PNC

1-2. Annual Supply/Demand Balance in Japanese Plutonium through the Year 2010

Year	Demand		Reprocessed Plutonium Supply			
	Reactors	Amount in tons	Tokai[e]	Rokkashomura[f]	Contracted Overseas Services[g]	Total in Tons
Present to 2005	PNC Fugen Joyo Monju	0.6–0.8[a]	0.4	—	0.2–0.4[h]	0.6–0.8
2005 to 2010	PNC	0.6–0.8	0.2	4.8	2.0	7.0
	FNR	0.7[b]				
	ATR	0.5[c]				
	LWR	5.0[d]				
	Total	7.0				

[a] Specific demand for PNC reactors Fugen, Joyo, and Monju.
[b] FNR = fast neutron reactor. The demonstration reactor program has been tentatively fixed. The plant size is 660 megawatts, and the construction will start several years after the year 2000.
[c] The demonstration ATR is expected to go into operation a few years after the year 2000.
[d] Producing no more than ten percent of Japan's total demand for LWR fuels.
[e] The Tokai plant will operate as usual to reprocess about 80 tons of spent fuel per year until the Rokkashomura plant starts full-scale operation.
[f] At the Rokkashomura plant, the small-scale hot operation is expected to start around the year 2000, and the full-scale operation will start around the year 2005.
[g] The major uncertainty associated with the availability of plutonium recovered from the overseas reprocessing services contracted is the MOX fuel fabrication service availability in Europe.
[h] Until the Rokkashomura plant starts full-scale operation, some of the PNC demand are to be met by plutonium from overseas reprocessing.

reactors Fugen (prototype advanced thermal reactor), Joyo (experimental fast reactor), and Monju (prototype fast reactor) will not meet the PNC's annual needs. The corporation needs some 0.6 to 0.8 tons of fissile plutonium annually(more than is expected from the Tokai plant, which will be put into use for purposes of research and development after the Rokkashomura plant has come into operation. Foreign supplies of plutonium will have to be relied on to make up for the shortage. It was for the purpose of refueling Monju that approximately 1 ton of fissile plutonium was returned to Japan from France on board a ship in early 1993 amid much publicity.

Japan Nuclear Fuel, Ltd., is preparing to build another reprocessing plant at Rokkashomura. The reprocessing capacity of the plant will be raised step by step to allow its operators enough time to gain experience. After several years of practice, they will be reprocessing 800 tons of spent fuel annually. The annual reprocessing capacity of 800 tons is the plant's limit, since it is all that the regulatory authority has approved. Table 1-2 shows that some 4.8 tons of fissile plutonium will be recovered annually from those 800 tons of spent fuel. Constant recovery of the 4.8 tons of plutonium from the reprocessing plant will not take place until sometime around 2005, when the demonstration fast neutron reactor and advanced thermal reactor are expected to come into operation. These reactors will combine with the three PNC reactors to claim some 40 percent (~1.8 tons) of all fissile plutonium recovered at Rokkashomura with the remaining 60 percent (~3.0 tons) scheduled for recycling in LWRs.

In addition, a majority of the plutonium reprocessed by foreign contractors for Japan is to be sent to a fuel fabrication plant in Europe for assembly into mixed oxide (MOX) fuel, combining plutonium and uranium, before it is returned to Japan for recycling in LWRs. That is the basic policy followed by Japan's electric utilities. Thus, how much plutonium will be shipped to Japan, and when it will be shipped, depends largely on reprocessing schedules and on the operation of MOX fuel-fabrication plants in Europe in the years ahead. Foreign reprocessing contractors will be commissioned to supply a cumulative total of about 30 tons of fissile plutonium based on estimates of the quantities of spent fuel already under contract with them. If those 30 tons of plutonium can all be returned over the period envisaged (through the year 2010), an average of 2 tons of fissile plutonium will be made available annually. As a rule, this will be recycled in Japanese LWRs.

THE ECONOMICS OF PLUTONIUM

Some opponents of the reliance on plutonium in Japan cast doubts on the economics of its use. Does it really have an economic advantage? What does Japan think the economics of plutonium are? These are very important questions.

Foreign criticisms or fears of Japan's program are partly related to allegations of its possible contribution to nuclear proliferation. But it may be the economic point of view that weighs more heavily with foreign critics. These critics might not be as adamant as they are against the Japanese program for the peaceful use of plutonium if they were persuaded of its economic reasonableness. In other words, they do not find it to be economically justified. They therefore wonder why then Japan is pushing ahead with its plutonium utilization program.

In explaining the economic rationale of the peaceful uses of plutonium, I have often made reference in the past several years to the costs of removing sulfur oxide (de-SOx) and nitrous oxide (de-NOx) emissions from thermal power plants. Obviously, the thermal power plants would be operated at a lower cost without removing these pollutants for the sake of environmental protection. Whether the cost of environmental protection is reasonable or not depends on how it compares with the electricity rate and how much of this cost can be passed on to consumers. For example, the recovery of carbon dioxide is a matter of controversial opinion now, as it is subject to a diverse range of provisional estimates. Most calculations put its cost at about 10 yen per kilowatt-hour. (The exchange rate averaged 107 yen per dollar in April 1996.) This is obviously too high because it doubles the cost of electric power. By contrast, one or two yen per kilowatt-hour is the cost to a plant if it is equipped with de-SOx and de-NOx devices only. This is reasonable enough for a plant to take the trouble to clean up the air, and almost all Japanese thermal power stations have this equipment. An international comparison of emissions of SOx and NOx from power stations is shown in Table 1-3.[5]

The reprocessing and recycling of spent fuel in Japan means that the fuel will not be left going to waste but will be put to efficient use through recycling. This will be one form of environmental protection. Its cost, according to my provisional estimates, is not more than 1 yen per kilowatt-hour (perhaps about 0.5 yen per kilowatt-

1-3. Emissions of Sulfur Oxide (SOx) and Nitrous Oxide (NOx) from Power Stations in 1989 (unit: 10^3 tons)

Country	SOx	NOx
United States	14,680	6,860
Japan	192[a]	200[a]
France	379[b]	112[b]
Germany	4,449	783
U.K.	2,640	769

[a] Average cost increments for de-SOx and de-NOx in Japanese fossil-fuel-fired power stations are 1 to 2 yen per kilowatt-hour.
[b] Mainly owing to its large share of electricity from nuclear-power sources.

hour. That will not be too much of a burden to bear. The breakdown of my cost estimates is given in table 1-4, in which the case of plutonium recycling in LWRs is used in order to make a provisional estimate of the per–kilowatt-hour cost of plutonium use.[6] Table 1-5 is shown in order to compare the basic cost data assumed to those employed in an Organization for Economic Cooperation and Development, Nuclear Energy Agency study.[7]

In table 1-4, let us first find out how much the recycling-based conservation of resources will contribute in the way of cost savings

1-4. Economics of Reprocessing and Recycling
(1/3 core MOX use at 1,000 MWe LWR in 2000–2020)

Natural Uranium Savings
180ton/yr/3 = 60ton/yr, ¥10^7/ton • 60ton/yr = ¥6 • 10^2/yr

Enrichment Service (Separative Work Unit = SWU) Savings
150tonSWU/yr/3 = 50tonSWU/yr, ¥10^7/tonSWU • 50tonSWU/yr = ¥5 • 10^2/yr

Enriched Uranium (EU) Fuel Fabrication Cost Savings
30ton/yr/3 = 10ton/yr, ¥5 • 10^7ton • 10ton/yr = ¥5 • 10^2/yr

Total Cost Savings
(¥6 + ¥5 + ¥5) • 10^2/yr ≈ ¥1.5 • 10^9/yr

Break-Even Cost of MOX Fuel Fabrication
¥1.5 • 10^9/yr/10tonMOX/yr ≈ ¥1.5 • 10^2/tonMOX

Reprocessing Cost
¥2 ~ 3 • 10^2/tonSF • 800tonSF/yr ≈ ¥1.6 ~ 2.4 • 10^{11}/yr
per kWh cost, averaged over total nuclear electricity expected in 2000 ~ 2020
¥1.6 ~ 2.4 • 10^{11}/yr/(60GWe • 7,000hr/yr) ≈ ¥0.4 ~ 0.6/kWh
cf. average cost of nuclear electricity in Japan ≈ ¥10/kWh

1-5.   Cost Estimates Assumed

	Suzuki	OECD/NEA[a]
Natural Uranium	$¥10^4$/kg U	$50/kg U
Enrichment	$¥10^4$/kg SWU	$110/kg SWU
EU Fabrication	$¥5 • 10^4$/kg U	$275/kg U
MOX Fuel Fabrication	$¥15 • 10^4$/kg MOX	$1,100/kg MOX
Reprocessing	$¥20 \sim 30 • 10^4$/kg U	ECU 722/kg U

[a] See endnote 7 of this chapter.

if calculated on the basis of annual fuel requirements for a 1,000 megawatt nuclear-power plant. Since the LWR program of recycling calls for the use of MOX fuel, in many cases in quantities equal to some one-third of total requirements, one will see a savings of some 600 million yen ($5.6 million) per year worth of natural uranium, some 500 million yen ($4.67 million) per year in enrichment service, and some 500 million yen ($4.67 million) per year in the fabrication costs of uranium fuel—totaling about 1,600,000,000 yen per year ($14.9 million).

The fabrication cost of MOX fuel, on the other hand, is a matter of conjecture, because it depends considerably on the scale of plant capacity and experience. Assuming the cost to be equal to the amount of fuel saved, it works out at some 150,000 yen ($1,401) per kilogram of MOX fuel—approximately three times as much as the fabrication cost of uranium fuel. On the basis of experience in Europe,[8] it would appear that cost penalties incurred by the fabrication of MOX fuel would be no more than what could be offset by the resulting conservation of uranium.

The question is what should be the point of view from which to assess the reprocessing cost as a prerequisite to recycling. If the issue is whether all spent fuel should be reprocessed or not, it is necessary to compare how much it costs when reprocessed with how much it would cost if not reprocessed. Even though it is, in reality, reprocessed in the case of Japan, such a comparison underlies many of the criticisms offered on recycling from an economic point of view. In Japan, the reprocessing cost is now on the order of 200 to 300 million yen ($1.86 to 2.8 million) per ton of spent fuel—or roughly about 1 yen per kilowatt-hour. On the other hand, if spent fuel is not reprocessed but is instead kept in storage for some time, it will involve a tiny fraction of the cost of reprocessing. Thus, there is a difference of about 1 yen per kilowatt-hour between the generation cost that spent fuel involves when reprocessed and the cost while it is not reprocessed but is stored.

The recycling of resources in many cases involves a greater cost than otherwise would be incurred. The crux of the debate is whether or not it can be justified as a necessary cost to protect the environment and to assure a wider choice of technology for the future. If the cost can be taken for granted as necessary, then it will still be important to determine how much of the spent fuel should be reprocessed at a given time and how much should remain unreprocessed and kept in storage.

What will be the outlook for the present Japanese program if it is looked at from this point of view? The reprocessing plant now under construction at Rokkashomura will be in full operation prior to the year 2000, when Japanese nuclear-power plants are expected to be generating a total of more than 400 billion kilowatt-hours of electricity. If the plants can get their spent fuel reprocessed at 200 million yen ($1.86 million) per ton, for instance, they will bear an average cost of about 0.4 yen per kilowatt-hour. Assuming the reprocessing costs go up to 300 million yen ($2.8 million) per ton, the plants will pay about 0.6 yen per kilowatt-hour.

As I mentioned already, this seems to be acceptable to those responsible for power generation as part of the cost they have to bear in order to provide the nation with energy security with a wide choice of technology and to assure the long-term protection of natural resources. In this connection, it should be noted that most of Japan's large thermal power plants of 150 megawatts and over are unexceptionably equipped with de-SOx and de-NOx devices, with the understanding that they pay 1-2 yen per kilowatt-hour as their share of the cost of the equipment.[9] These high levels of cost-bearing are the reason that no countries are more advanced than Japan in the abatement method of SOx and NOx. But the Japanese consider it worth their while to pay that much for de-SOx and de-NOx if it assures them environmental protection. One important meaning of reprocessing is in its contribution toward putting radioactive wastes under appropriate management. I would think that environmental protection is also an important factor in considering the economic rationale for reprocessing.

To sum up, the economic question to be considered is not simply whether the cost of reprocessing is low or high by comparison.

It might be advisable to regard it as the cost of environmental protection and to approach it from the standpoint of how much of this cost consumers can be asked to pay.

Needless to say, another important point is that the cost of recycling should not be left as high as it is. The cost should be made more economical in the future. In this respect, as in others already discussed, it is important to think in the long term.

HOW CAN JAPAN PROMOTE NUCLEAR DISARMAMENT?

What do Japanese technologies for the peaceful uses of nuclear energy have to do with cooperation toward nuclear disarmament? In my view, there are two ways in which Japan could contribute to disarmament.

For one thing, I personally think that it might be advisable to see that Japanese technologies for the peaceful uses of plutonium, which are considerably advanced, are offered positively by Japan for application in finding effective uses for the plutonium released from dismantled nuclear weapons. This would be a fine international contribution. For example, the Japanese could help convert plutonium from dismantled nuclear weapons into MOX fuel for nuclear reactors. It would be desirable for the Japanese government to take a positive step in this direction.

Plutonium from dismantled nuclear weapons will contribute substantially to nuclear disarmament if it has some value added. For example, a relatively easy solution has been found for the release of highly enriched uranium from dismantled nuclear weapons, because the methods for this release realize the profit that can be expected from it. In other words, they produce some value added. For the release of plutonium as well, reassuring and reliable Japanese technologies and methods could be offered as part of a possible international agreement, or in response to international requests for a positive Japanese contribution.

In April 1994, the Japanese prototype fast-breeder reactor at Monju reached its initial nuclear chain reaction. As an article in one well-known American newspaper noted:

> Environmental groups—particularly foreign ones—have taken issue with Japan's nuclear power program, both for its devel-

opment of breeder reactors that would increase the world's plutonium glut and for shipping a ton of plutonium by sea from France to Japan in late 1992 and early 1993 for use as fuel in the breeder reactor. Mindful of such criticism, Japanese officials are stressing another aspect of the breeder reactor concept: With some design changes, a reactor like the Monju can be made to consume rather than breed plutonium. If that is possible, breeder reactors might be beneficial to the United States and other countries saddled with plutonium supplies that nobody has found a good way to dispose of.[10]

Indeed, it is true that a fast reactor can become either a breeder or a burner of plutonium. As a burner, Monju could help deal with the excess of plutonium arising from dismantled nuclear weapons.

At the same time, Japan should play a more positive role in the current active international efforts to promote nuclear non-proliferation and the elimination of nuclear weapons. For example, in international inspection activities, we need a technology that will enable us to find out whether a certain solution or a certain waste contains plutonium. Precision-measurement devices and equipment that may serve these purposes can be developed only through advanced technologies. Such technologies will also be needed to enable computers to determine what is necessary to prevent nuclear proliferation.

If Japan has such technologies—and I believe such technologies will certainly become available—they could be used in advance to prevent problems conducive to nuclear proliferation from developing in other countries where a proliferation danger exists.

Another important point is that Japan, as an Asian country, has a responsibility to extend nuclear cooperation to other parts of Asia. In East Asia, for example, North Korea is under nuclear suspicion. I do not know if North Korea really has nuclear weapons. If it has, the question of how Japan should face this situation is a difficult one. This case illustrates, in any event, that the time has come for Asians to discuss how they can promote the peaceful uses of nuclear energy in such a way that they can reassure one another. It would be most undesirable to keep some specific country in isolation.

There was a time when a delicate political balance could be maintained between North and South Korea, with backing from the Soviet Union and the United States, respectively. But the end of the Cold War structure led South Korea to establish diplomatic relations with China, probably leaving North Korea with a profound feeling of isolation. The balance of power in East Asia has entered a new phase.

It is an important reality that the development of nuclear energy has begun in China, is making steady progress in South Korea, and is far advanced in Taiwan. Japan, of course, is Asia's most advanced nuclear-energy state. At the same time, conditions are growing for the introduction of nuclear power in Indonesia and the Philippines, and eventually in Thailand. Therefore, it is important that a framework of cooperation for the peaceful uses of nuclear energy be set up, as was the case with the European Atomic Energy Community (EURATOM), although it would be difficult to build the same type of mechanism in Asia. The establishment of such a framework would enable Asian countries to have their researchers keep contact with each other and to establish reliable rules within which they can feel free to go ahead with their development projects.

Ideas should be developed for setting up something like EURATOM in East Asia to promote the organic and steady development of international nuclear cooperation for peaceful purposes. Such a framework might be extended to include Australia, too. Setting up an "organization for Pacific Basin nuclear cooperation" is one idea. It could be opened up to entry by the United States and Canada, and possibly by Russia.

IN REPLY TO THE CRITICS

Japan's plan to use plutonium mixed with uranium to generate electricity has caused much misunderstanding and created many misconceptions. Many criticize the plan in the belief that plutonium is a deadly substance, but this view is scientifically unfounded. Radium emits more alpha radiation than does plutonium, but hot springs that contain radium in their water pose no hazard to guests who frequent such spas. Plutonium is quite safe in small quantities and at low density, as is radium. Utmost care must naturally be taken to ensure safety at nuclear facilities and scientific laboratories where radium or plutonium is used in a concentrated form. The danger of handling high concentrations of these substances is clear; Marie Curie, the chemist who discovered radium, ultimately died from overexposure to it. But in view of the stringent safety standards that have now been established, based on all the experience accumulated on the uses of uranium and plutonium worldwide, these risks do not warrant unnecessary concern.

Table 1-6[11] illustrates the radiological hazard of plutonium as compared with uranium and radium. As far as the annual-intake limit is concerned, the ingestion hazard of radium is about 300 times more than that of plutonium. The seriousness of this hazard has been spelled out in an American study:

> The Curies' discovery of radium, for example, kicked off the Milk Radium Therapy movement among American socialites, and precipitated a lucrative trade in radium-based belts, hearing aids, toothpaste, face cream, and hair tonic. Most lucrative of all was Radiothor, a glow-in-the-dark mineral water that promised a cure for more than 150 maladies. The Federal Trade Commission, ever vigilant, cracked down on competing portions that lacked advertised levels of radioactivity. The steel mogul, socialite, and amateur golf champion Evan MacBurney Byers faithfully drank Radiothor every day from 1926 to 1931. By the latter year he had developed cancer of the jaw, a presumed but unproved consequence of the radiation. He died miserably in 1932. This well-publicized incident alerted the public to the dangers of ionizing radiation, and helped spur much-needed government action.[12]

Some people may wonder why Japan is proceeding with a plan to use plutonium at a time when other countries are abandoning similar policies as being economically unattractive. As I mentioned already, one of the main reasons lies in the difficulty of disposing of highly radioactive spent fuel from nuclear-power generation. For instance, the United States, which is endowed with vast land area and many geologically stable zones, has attempted to eliminate such waste by burying it deep in the ground. However, this method is not always possible for a small, earthquake-prone country like Japan. Another concern centers on the adverse effects of buried waste on the environment. In this regard, the Japanese plan, under which plu-

1-6. Radiological Hazard of Plutonium (Pu)

	Half life (years)	Specific Radioactivity (Pu = 1)	Annual Limit of Intake (Pu = 1)	
			Ingestion	Inhalation
Uranium	$7 \cdot 10^8$ to $4.5 \cdot 10^9$	$3 \cdot 10^{-5}$ to $5 \cdot 10^{-6}$	$\sim 10^4$	$\sim 10^5$
Plutonium	$\sim 2.4 \cdot 10^4$	1	1	1
Radium	$1.6 \cdot 10^3$	15	$\sim 1/300$	~ 2

tonium is recovered from spent fuel, would contribute substantially to mitigating the burden on the environment.

Turning to the cost-effectiveness of the Japanese plan, while it is true that the world prices of uranium are declining and it would seem of no economic benefit to use plutonium, which is more expensive, the cost difference between the use of the two kinds of fuel for nuclear-power generation in Japan, as illustrated already, amounts to less than 10 percent. This should be justifiable from the public viewpoint, since the use of plutonium is more conducive to environmental preservation. To cite a case in point, almost all present thermoelectric plants in Japan have had to install de-SOx and de-NOx devices to abate environmental pollution, and the cost of these devices accounts for about 10-20 percent of the total cost of power generation.

Japanese plans to begin operating a prototype fast reactor and to construct a "demonstration plant" to prove the commercial feasibility of reprocessing also have been questioned on the grounds of economic efficiency and safety. Yet the suspicious are ignorant of the realities of nuclear-power generation. At present, nuclear power supplies about one-third of the electrical energy generated in the member states of the Organisation for Economic Co-operation and Development. Nuclear energy enabled the world to wean itself from the excessive dependence on oil that invited the oil crises of the 1970s. Light-water reactor technology has matured in terms of both economic efficiency and safety, and the same progress can be achieved in the realm of fast-reactor technology if projects are carried out steadily. But innovation cannot be attained without initiatives.

Some may ask why Japan is trying to increase its plutonium supply capacity at a time when the world already has a surplus. First, the grade of plutonium for military use should be distinguished from that for civilian use. Second, the surplus plutonium around the world is not necessarily available internationally, since its trade is restricted. What is even more significant is a comparison of the amount of plutonium held by individual countries. In this respect, the former Soviet Union has by far the greatest amount of plutonium. In addition to its surplus civilian-use plutonium, approximately a 100–metric ton surplus of military-use plutonium is being created as a by-product of disarmament agreements between the United States and Russia.[13]   The amount of civilian-use plutonium to be used under the Japanese plan cannot be compared with the military-use plutonium remaining in the former Soviet Union. Japan is promoting the use of plutonium as part of the management of its own spent fuel. Even so, Japan should feel obligated to extend as much assistance as it can to the former Soviet Union in order to give further impetus to nuclear disarmament.

Finally, some argue that the further use of plutonium by Japan will increase the risk of nuclear proliferation by encouraging other nations to advance similar plans. The risk of nuclear proliferation in other countries does exist, but it is irrelevant in the case of the Japanese plans to use plutonium for peaceful purposes. The civilian use of plutonium is not of industrial value unless it generates a substantial amount of electricity, as is intended in Japan. It would make no economic sense for countries with few nuclear power plants to utilize plutonium for their energy needs. However, to ensure a better understanding concerning its use of plutonium, it is important for Japan to make every effort to enhance the transparency of its nuclear-energy plans, so as to dispel global concern over nuclear proliferation.

Actually, the Science and Technology Agency in Japan disclosed the amount of the Japanese plutonium stockpile, both domestic and overseas. This is shown in Table 1-7.[14] Japan is the first and only country that has on its own initiative disclosed information concerning its long-term program of plutonium use and its own actual stockpile of plutonium.

1-7.   Plutonium Balance in Japan, as of December 1992 (kilograms)

Supply Source	Recovered	Purchased	Returned	Transfered	Reused	Stored[a]
Tokai, Japan	2,925	—	—	(+1,060)	2,430	1,555
COGEMA (France)	3,260	5	1,255	(-1,060)	195	2,010
BNFL (U.K.)	1,560	320	980	—	980	900
United States	—	100	100	—	100	—
Germany	—	60	60	—	60	—
Total	7,745	485	2,335		3,765	4,465

[a] Stored = (recovered + purchased + transfered) – (returned or reused).
Note: 1,000 kilograms = one metric ton.
Source: Science and Technology Agency, 1993.

PAST AND FUTURE

A Pulitzer Prize–winning laureate, Richard Rhodes, gave a very impressive talk titled "The New Morning of the World" at the 27th Annual Conference of the Japan Atomic Industrial Forum, held at Hiroshima, April 13, 1994.[15] I was deeply impressed and totally agree with what he said there.

Rhodes first introduced the fact that, immediately after the discovery of how to release nuclear energy, the great Danish physicist Niels Bohr made his utmost endeavor to stop the creation of "a weapon of unparalleled power." In particular, Bohr emphasized that common security against the nuclear threat requires transparency; a nuclear-free world will have to be completely transparent where nuclear technology is concerned. Rhodes cited Bohr's lecture given before the United Nations in 1950:

> An open world, where each nation can assert itself solely by the extent to which it can contribute to the common culture and is able to help others with experience and resources must be the goal to put above everything else. . . . The very fact that knowledge is itself the basis for civilization points directly to openness as the way to overcome the present crisis.

Rhodes then touched upon the goal of science, referring to Bohr's idea, defining it as "the gradual removal of prejudices." As a matter of fact, science has gradually removed the prejudice that there is a limited amount of energy available in the world to concentrate into explosives and that it is possible to accumulate more of such energy than one's enemies and thereby militarily to prevail.

In this context, Rhodes mentioned that today we seem to have come to a turning point in the history of the application of nuclear energy, the leveling-off of the first step of the learning curve. One of our concerns about nuclear proliferation today relates to what is happening now in North Korea. Rhodes, however, argues that the diminished third wave of nuclear-weapons development that is now proceeding, particularly in East Asia, is not likely to rise as steeply or to continue for as long as the first superpower arms race; this is because the world knows more now than it knew then, including its knowledge of the economic waste and the ultimate futility of piling up nuclear arms. What we have learned from the past is that the first great historical consequence of the discovery of how to release nuclear energy has been to limit national sovereignty and to forestall world war—and that the next great consequence, already ongoing, will be to add significantly to human welfare by increasing sustainable energy resources and decreasing pollution.

Rhodes went on to elucidate the role of nuclear energy from a global perspective, and I totally agree with his opinion:

> Satisfying human aspirations is what our species invents technology to do. Some people, secure in comfortable affluence, may dream of a simpler and smaller world. However noble such a dream appears to be, its hidden agenda is elitist, selfish and violent. Millions of children die every year in the world for lack of adequate resources—clean water, food, medical care— and the development of those resources is directly dependent on energy supplies. The real world of real human beings needs more energy, not less. As oil and coal continue their historic decline, that energy across the next half-century will necessarily come from nuclear power and natural gas.

There are a number of people who fear the diversion of plutonium in a nuclear-power economy. In this connection, Rhodes placed emphasis on the necessity of more objective and careful discussion, noting that the critics should look more carefully at the historical patterns of horizontal proliferation and the behavior of terrorists. He pointed out that Iraq turned to the electromagnetic separation of uranium, a technique that the United States abandoned at the end of the World War II. What is suggested by this fact, he said, is that nations bent on developing a nuclear-weapons capability will find a way to do so, whether that way is one that may be used for peaceful purposes in other countries or not. In other words, nuclear proliferation is more of a political than a technical problem. In addition, it is Rhodes's view that terrorists have shown little inclination or ability to add nuclear engineers and metallurgists to their ranks. An example he cited is that the weapons of choice in the bombing of New York's World Trade Center were nitrate fertilizer and fuel oil, which the terrorists found easy to purchase in a foreign country and were confident they knew how to ignite.

With the demise of the former Soviet Union and its replacement by a volatile but resourceful collective of new states, Rhodes believes that we are already moving to a new level of world security with reduced numbers of nuclear weapons and—what is equally valuable—extended response times for the arsenals that remain. Certainly we will not easily find our way to a world free of nuclear

65

weapons, and it will also be necessary to pursue major reductions in conventional armaments. In considering the impact of the end of the Cold War on the peaceful uses of nuclear power in the future, it is very important for Japan to be aware of international trends regarding nuclear disarmament. Adjusting, during the last five decades, to the new knowledge about how to release nuclear energy has put us at no little risk. But I share Rhodes's opinion that the evident uselessness of nuclear weapons may bring that millennium to an end sooner rather than later. He concluded his talk by saying the end of the Cold War surely counts as the new morning of the world.

CONCLUSION

The severity of the economic difficulties and international challenges facing Japan makes it difficult to predict how the development of nuclear energy can be promoted from a long-range point of view. The commercialization of fast reactors is not expected in the near future, but the reprocessing of spent fuel needs to be promoted, since spent fuel has to be kept under proper management. This being the case, for the time being, Japan has no choice but to keep within the limits of a steady program for the use of plutonium in LWRs. Perhaps this is the most realistic line of policy that Japan can now pursue.

These days, I feel increasing numbers of people connected with the Japanese nuclear program have the idea that things will take their natural course. This idea, however, will not lead them to make the hard choices required by the bitter realities that confront them. I am sure that there are others who agree with this critical assessment. I earnestly hope that the time will come when the pursuit of a long-term program in Japan brings it in ten to twenty years to a level perceptibly more progressive in the way of environmental security. What is most important now, I would say, is to know how to bring about a successful combination of the Occidental practice of short-range reasoning with the Oriental practice of long-range reasoning. Such a harmony will possibly be established in Japan, because that is the approach that Japan has already brought to many aspects of its modernization.[16]

Finally, I might say that the critical issue relating to plutonium is not how plutonium will maintain its existence but whether or not further technical skills will be developed in the use of plutonium.

Some are apparently arguing in the belief that there would be no problems if only plutonium ceased to exist. I would say this kind of argument will get nowhere. Science and technology are things written indelibly on everybody's mind. The history of civilization shows that mankind has faced great difficulties and crises. But they have been surmounted, it should be noted, through the introduction of new sciences and technologies, not because of the existence or non-existence of any material.

NOTES

[1]H. Etherington, ed., *Nuclear Engineering Handbook* (New York: McGraw-Hill, 1958).

[2]A. Suzuki, "A More Flexible Program to Make Civil Use of Plutonium" (in Japanese), *Energy Forum*, 337:1, 1983, pp. 50(51.

[3]A. Suzuki, "Forming Japan's Sustainable Program for Peaceful Use of Nuclear Energy" (in Japanese), *Energy Forum*, 365:5, 1985, pp. 37(41.

[4]Atomic Energy Commission, Japan, "Long-Term Program for Research, Development and Utilization of Nuclear Energy," June 1995.

[5]Organisation for Economic Co-operation and Development, "OECD Environmental Data," 1993, pp. 17(23.

[6]A. Suzuki, "Burning Actinides and Long-lived Fission Products - A Japanese Perspective," presented at the NATO Workshop on Managing the Plutonium Surplus: Applications and Options, London, January 25, 1994.

[7]Organisation for Economic Co-operation and Development, Nuclear Energy Agency, "The Economics of the Nuclear Fuel Cycle," Committee for Technical and Economic Studies on Nuclear Energy Development and the Fuel Cycle (NDC), June 1993.

[8]P. Verbeek, "Destination of Warhead Plutonium: A Western European Electrical Utility Viewpoint," presented at the 27th Annual Conference of the Japan Atomic Industrial Forum, Hiroshima, April 13, 1994.

[9]J. Ando, "The State of the Arts of Off-Gas Treatment Technologies in the World" (in Japanese), Institute of Coal Technology, Tokyo, August 1990.

[10]T. R. Reid, "Reactor Start-up Fuels Japan's Energy Plans," *The Washington Post*, April 6, 1993.

[11]Science and Technology Agency, "Upper Bound on Quantity of Radioisotope, Derived from Annual Limit of Intake" (in Japanese), *Japan Isotope Association*, March 1994.

[12]K. R. Foster, D. E. Bernstein, and P. W. Huber, eds., *Phantom Risks: Scientific Inference and the Law* (Cambridge: MIT Press, 1993), pp. 23-24.

[13]D. Albright, F. Berkhout, and W. Walker, *World Inventory of Plutonium and Highly-Enriched Uranium* (Oxford: Oxford University Press, 1993).

[14]Science and Technology Agency, "On the Plutonium Supply and Demand in Japan" (in Japanese), October 1993.

[15]R. Rhodes, "The New Morning of the World," presented at the 27th Annual Conference of the Japan Atomic Industrial Forum, Hiroshima, April 13, 1994.

[16]A. Suzuki, "Japanese Nuclear Policy in a Changing World," presented at the 18th International Symposium held by the Uranium Institute, London, September 10, 1993.

CHAPTER 2

JAPAN'S PLUTONIUM PROGRAM: A CRITICAL REVIEW

JINZABURO TAKAGI

INTRODUCTION

As early as 1944, Enrico Fermi warned, in relation to the future of nuclear energy, that the public might not accept an energy source that produces both an enormous amount of radioactive waste and materials that could be made into nuclear weapons.[1] Now, fifty years after Fermi's warning, the proliferation of and environmental risks posed by the "essential nuclear material," plutonium, arouse renewed worldwide concern as vast quantities of plutonium are to be taken out of dismantled nuclear weapons in Russia and the United States, and as surplus plutonium is generated through civilian reprocessing programs in Japan and other countries.

On June 24, 1994, after protracted debate, the Japan Atomic Energy Commission (JAEC) disclosed its new, revised version of the Long-Term Program for the Development and Utilization of Nuclear Energy originally adopted in 1987.

There had been press speculation that the ambitious 1987 plutonium program was being drastically scaled down in the revision as a result of international criticism and concern. But it is now clear that the plan has been set back by some 10 years only, and the projected plutonium demand and supply level by the year 2010 will be "reduced" to 100 to 110 tons (all plutonium amounts are given in total plutonium base, not in fissile plutonium base) from the original plan of 110 to 130 tons.[2] This is simply an adjustment of the old program due to unavoidable technical delays; therefore, the essence of Japan's plutonium policy has not been changed.

The revised program states that "Japan intends to carry forward the development and utilization of nuclear energy in strict conformance with the principle of peaceful use only" and "to redouble its effort with respect to winning international confidence concerning the non-proliferation of nuclear weapons." However, when we look into the details of what is actually taking place in the Japanese nuclear program, it is not so easy to be optimistic concerning its "peacefulness."

THE DANGER OF A PLUTONIUM SURPLUS

As in Europe, a large plutonium surplus is expected in Japan. In 1992, William Dircks, then Deputy Director General of the International Atomic Energy Agency (IAEA), stated at the annual meeting of the Japan Atomic Industry Forum:

> Even if one disregards the fissile material from nuclear warheads, the excess of isolated fissile plutonium from civilian nuclear programs poses a major political and security problem worldwide.
>
> As a result of nuclear fuel reprocessing, and potentially as a result of nuclear weapons dismantling, in the foreseeable future the supply of plutonium will far exceed the industrial capacity to absorb plutonium into peaceful, commercial nuclear industrial activities.[3]

The Japanese government's stated policy on plutonium supply and demand is that it does not and will not stockpile excess plutonium. This policy was most clearly expressed in 1992 by Toichi Sakata, then Director of the Nuclear Fuel Division, Science and Technology Agency (STA):

> Therefore, it is a sheer misunderstanding that Japan is accumulating a huge amount of plutonium, and we do not expect any situation under which plutonium without a definite use would be accumulated in this country.
>
> It should be noted here that Japan's plutonium utilization program is to proceed keeping the supply and demand in balance, not only in terms of the long-term cumulative inventory, but also on a year-to-year basis. Thus even the temporary accumulation of a surplus in Japan is not conceivable.[4]

What is actually happening in Japan, however, appears to mark a deviation from this no-surplus policy. According to the cumulative plutonium supply and demand figures made public by the STA in October 1993, Japan's plutonium surplus had already amounted to 6.3 tons as of the end of 1992. Of this 6.3-ton surplus, 2.2 tons was stockpiled in Japan, while the remaining 4.1 tons was stored at European reprocessing facilities.

In November 1994, the JAEC published an updated plutonium inventory as of the end of 1993 that has aroused renewed concern over the surplus plutonium that Japan has accumulated. A breakdown of these figures on the basis of individual reactors is presented in table 2-1. Supply and demand data through 1993 is summarized in table 2-2.

STA figures released in November 1995 show a total plutonium inventory of 13.1 tons at the end of 1994, of which 11.6 tons can be regarded as surplus, implying a 2.8 ton increase in the surplus in 1994 alone. While most of this increase is attributable to reprocessing in Europe, the stockpile in Japan also went up.

The prospect at the beginning of 1996 was for a still bigger surplus—perhaps as large as 25 million tons by the turn of the century. Even before the Monju reactor accident in December 1995, there were delays in the fast-breeder reactor (FBR) project, and the Monju accident will mean greater delays. The most optimistic prediction is that it will take from three to four years for Monju to restart. The government says that the plutonium stored for use in Monju will be used in the Joyo experimental FBR, but the expected annual demand by the Joyo and Fugen reactors together is less than 0.2 tons. Another factor adding to the surplus will be the public questioning of the safety of the plutonium-based nuclear program aroused by the Monju accident. The government program envisages the use of plutonium in reactors in a combination with uranium known as mixed oxide (MOX) fuel. But opposition to the use of this fuel has grown in the areas where the reactors are located since the accident.

It is also worth noting that, although Japan carried out the 1992 shipment of plutonium from France, claiming that it urgently needed the plutonium to fuel the Monju reactor, not all of the plutonium transported to Japan had been used prior to the Monju accident. While the Power Reactor and Nuclear Fuel Development Corporation (PNC) has said that it planned to use the remaining plutonium for the fabrication of MOX fuel for the first reloading of

2-1.   Japan's Separated Plutonium (Pu) Inventory (as of end of 1993)

Facility	Total Pu (kg.)	Stockpiles (s) or In Use/Ready for Use (u)
Reprocessing Plant	**326**	
as nitrate	288	s
as oxide	38	s
Fuel Fabrication	**3,269**	
stored in containers	2,339a	s
in test or process line	790	u
completed fuel	140	u
Reactor Site	**1,089**	
Joyo	15	u
Monju	637	u
Fugen	12	u
Critical assemblies	425	u
Overseas Reprocessors	**6,177**	
U.K. (BNFL)	1,266	s
France (COGEMA)	4,911	s
Total	**10,861**	8,842(s)+2,019(u)

aThis figure includes the 1,508 tons that were carried by *Akatsuki-maru* from France and remain unused.

2-2.   Annual Plutonium Supply and Demand for 1993

Supply		Demand	
From	Total Pu (kg.)	For	Total Pu (kg.)
Tokai Reprocessing Plant	421	**Monju and Fugen Fuel**	454
Abroad (COGEMA)	1,508		

2-3. Japan's Separated Plutonium (Pu) Inventory (as of end of 1994)

Facility	Total Pu (kg.)	Stockpiles (s) or In Use/Ready for Use (u)
Reprocessing Plant	**836**	
as nitrate	710	s
as oxide	126	s
Fuel Fabrication Plant	**3,018**	
stored as oxide	2,032	s
in test or processing line	948	u
completed fuel	38	u
Reactor Sites	**499**	
Joyo	6	u
Monju	15	u
Fugen	53	u
Critical assemblies	425	u
Overseas Reprocessors	**8,720**	
U.K. (BNFL)	1,412	s
France (COGEMA)	7,308	s
Total	**13,073**	11.588(s) +1.484(u)

[a] Attribution to u and s is the judgment of the author.
Source: Science and Technology Agency.

Monju, which was to have taken place in 1996 or 1997, inventory data and recent reprocessing performance[5] suggest that plutonium from the Tokai reprocessing plant alone would have been enough to fuel Monju, as well as the other two reactors (Fugen and Joyo) that use MOX fuel, until the turn of the century.

Due to technical difficulties and the large sums of money expected to be spent before the FBRs are commercialized (if ever), the utilities are now becoming more and more reluctant to invest in them. Accordingly, if the government follows its no-surplus policy, most of the 100-110 tons of plutonium resulting from reprocessing by the year 2010 will have to be consumed in light-water reactors (LWRs). This is the scenario the JAEC actually envisages. But the utilities are also reticent about large-scale MOX burning in LWRs because of the poor economics of MOX fuel. In addition, limited

2-4. Japan's Plutonium Supply and Demand

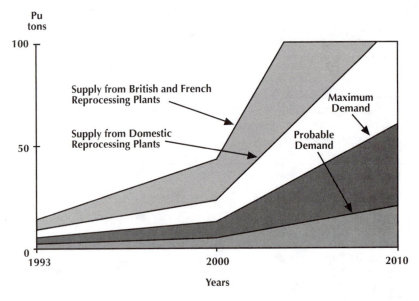

MOX fuel-fabrication capacities in European and Japanese MOX plants make the scenario extremely unrealistic. A vast plutonium surplus is unavoidable in Japan as in Europe, and I estimate that the cumulative surplus will grow to between 50 and 80 tons by the year 2010[6] (see figure 2-4).

PROLIFERATION AND DIVERSION RISKS

WEAPONS USABILITY OF REACTOR-GRADE PLUTONIUM

The nuclear-weapons usability of reactor-grade plutonium now seems to have been established internationally. In Japan, however, plutonium utilization proponents still persist in putting forward arguments to the effect that it is not practical to use reactor-grade plutonium, with its high level of contaminants, for nuclear weapons, and that it should therefore be considered a virtually non-usable material for weapons. Since this subject is emerging as a key issue in Japan, I would like to address it briefly here.

The weapons-usability of reactor-grade plutonium is discussed in the recently published report[7] of the National Academy of Sciences on the disposition of nuclear weapons:

> Virtually any combination of plutonium isotopes can be used to make a nuclear weapon.
>
> With reactor-grade plutonium, the probability of "pre-ignition" is very large. Pre-ignition can substantially reduce the explosive yield, since the weapon may blow itself apart and thereby cut short the chain reaction that releases the energy. Calculations demonstrate, however, that even if pre-ignition occurs at the worst possible moment, the explosive yield of a relatively simple device similar to the Nagasaki bomb would be on the order of one or a few kilotons.

That reactor-grade plutonium is weapons-usable was indeed proved in a test conducted in the United States in 1962.[8] According to a RAND report published in 1993,[9] the critical mass of reactor-grade plutonium is estimated to be merely 7 kilograms, which is only 40 percent more than that of weapons-grade plutonium. J. Carson Mark, former nuclear-weapons designer at Los Alamos, also points out[10] that the difficulties of developing an effective design of the most straightforward type are not appreciably greater with reactor-grade plutonium than are those with weapons-grade plutonium.

Despite these well-based arguments that reactor-grade plutonium is weapons-usable in the United States—where nuclear weapons were actually designed, produced, and tested—many influential Japanese nuclear-technology experts, such as Ryukichi Imai[11] and Hiroyoshi Kurihara,[12] have been arguing to the contrary without any evidence. Kurihara writes as follows:

> Many Japanese experts express the opinion that reactor-grade plutonium could not be used for workable nuclear weapons. If one wanted to produce a nuclear explosive device from reactor-grade plutonium, it would merely be a nuclear firework, producing a glare and big noise. It would not cause the big disastrous effects of nuclear bombs, including a very high temperature heat wave and shock wave as well as a large amount of fallout.

If Japan's plutonium management is really based on such a false theory, there is good reason to have concern over the proliferation of Japan's plutonium.

JAPAN'S NUCLEAR OPTION

Most Japanese people believe that Japan will undoubtedly stick to its non-nuclear-weapons position and abide by its Three Non-Nuclear Principles. But whether Japan will continue to be a non-nuclear-weapons state indefinitely is open to question. There were opportunities when Japan could have enacted a nuclear-free law. The so-called Three Non-Nuclear Principles (not to possess, produce, or introduce nuclear weapons) were first formulated by the Sato Administration in 1967 as government policy and included in a 1971 Diet resolution. Since the adoption of the resolution, there have been attempts to make the principle into a law, but these attempts have failed so far due to persistent opposition by conservative politicians—and the Ministry of Foreign Affairs—who are not willing to rule out legally the possibility of a nuclear option.

An unnamed high official of the Ministry of Foreign Affairs was quoted in 1992 by Asahi Shimbun[13] as saying:

> My personal opinion is that Japan should not abandon the nuclear option as backing for its diplomatic strength. Japan should possess a nuclear-weapons capability but keep the non-nuclear policy for the moment. For this reason, Japan should accumulate plutonium and develop rocket technology that can be converted to missiles.

The official's comment is remarkable in that he is hinting at Japan's stockpiling of plutonium as "a backing for Japan's diplomatic strength." Moreover, this opinion may not be isolated. Actually, a 1994 report in *Mainichi Shimbun*[14] revealed that a top-secret Foreign Ministry document in 1969 stated that Japan should retain its potential to build nuclear arms. I myself once heard a similar view from a Japanese diplomat. There are therefore good reasons to worry about Japan's future exercise of its nuclear option, though I don't believe that a secret nuclear-weapons program is currently under way in Japan.

Although Prime Ministers since 1993 have supported the indefinite extension of the NPT, the "nuclear option" issue continues to boil beneath the surface. For example, in a speech to the press,[15] Ichiro Ozawa, leader of the Shinshinto (New Frontier) Party, said that he is convinced that North Korea is already armed with nuclear weapons. While he did not elaborate, his remark is generally interpreted in Japan as suggesting that Japan should not necessarily rule out the nuclear option.

REGIONAL INSTABILITY

Japan's ambitious plutonium program is arousing worldwide suspicions that Japan may someday go nuclear. This concern over Japan's nuclear armament is particularly strong among Asian Pacific nations that had bitter experiences with Japan's past military invasions. In addition, the lack of economic justification for Japan's plutonium program strengthens the suspicion that the hidden aim of this program is to develop nuclear capabilities. The lack of transparency and democratic decision-making in Japan on nuclear issues may enhance the concern.

Already, North Korea points to Japan's plutonium program as a rationale for its own nuclear program. This shows that Japan's plutonium policy could trigger a chain reaction in the East Asian region. Remarks such as Ozawa's would surely stimulate Japanese opinion in favor of more preparedness against the North Korean nuclear threat, and this in turn would stimulate nuclear activities not only in North Korea but also in other Asian countries—notably China and South Korea. This kind of chain reaction would greatly destabilize the region and could eventually lead to a nuclear arms race.

The United States has successfully prevented South Korea, Taiwan, and other Asian countries from constructing reprocessing plants and has obtained North Korean assent—in the 1994 Agreed Framework—to scrap reprocessing. Yet, until now, it has acquiesced in Japan's full-scale plutonium program, including the recent approval of the construction of the Recycle Equipment Test Facility, which could be used to separate supergrade plutonium from the blanket fuel in the Monju reactor. This U.S. policy is patently discriminatory, and sooner or later it will become difficult for the United States to maintain such a discriminatory approach and for Japan to sustain its preferential status. In a discussion with the author, Toichi Sakata, the former head of the Science and Technology Agency, mentioned that a distinction should be made between "good countries" and "bad countries," and that bad countries should be prohibited by the international community from developing civilian plutonium programs. Apart from the discriminatory attitude exemplified by this kind of remark, which is typical of Japanese elite bureaucrats, such a distinction cannot be enforced. As a practical matter, if Japan's plutonium program proceeds as planned, other Asian nations will eventually follow suit with reprocessing programs. Indeed, it has been reported that China has already started construction of a major reprocessing plant.[16] This kind of "chain reaction" will unavoidably lead to regional nuclear proliferation, or at least fear of proliferation, which might then provoke Japan to embark on a nuclear-weapons program.

THE HOLD-UP ISSUE

Another issue that aroused international concern over Japan's plutonium program was the revelation of a large amount of plutonium "held-up" at the Tokai reactor. This issue came to light when the Nuclear Control Institute, a Washington-based public-interest organization, revealed an IAEA finding that as much as 70 kilograms of plutonium had accumulated inside a part of the reactor known as the "glove boxes" at Tokai. STA and PNC admitted that the problem had been pointed out by the IAEA and claimed that the plutonium was not the prohibited "material unaccounted for," but could be defined as "held-up" material.

The Tokai facility is renowned for possessing a highly advanced technology called the Glove Box Assessment System to monitor the small amount of plutonium that attaches to the insides of glove boxes with the use of a specialized fission neutron counting system. Despite this elaborate counting system, the nominal measurement error of the system is 10-15 percent. This indicates that, with a hold-up of 70 kilograms inside the glove boxes, more than 8 kilograms of plutonium (a "significant" quantity of plutonium as defined by the IAEA and enough to make one nuclear bomb) could be overlooked even if it were missing or elaborately diverted.

While PNC and STA claim that the hold-up has nothing to do with plutonium diversion, a *Nuclear Fuel* report[17] suggests that IAEA officials are not satisfied with the PNC-STA assurance of non-diversion and have demanded a complete account.

THE RUSSIAN CONNECTION

Japan's plutonium program encourages Russia to pursue a civilian plutonium program based on the utilization of plutonium from dismantled nuclear warheads. In Russia, many people inside the nuclear establishment regard plutonium from dismantled nuclear weapons as an asset or even a "treasure" and are in favor of using it as reactor fuel or selling it to overseas utilities for foreign currency.[18]

As the frequent visits to Japan of MINATOM's head, V. N. Mikhailov, show, the Russian government is willing to cooperate with Japan in bringing the dismantled plutonium into civilian use or in selling it to Japan as MOX. While Japanese utilities have not expressed an interest in using Russian plutonium, STA seems to be willing to help Russia construct fast reactors to dispose of weapons-grade plutonium.[19] STA's intention may also be to keep the Russian plutonium industry alive and to take advantage of the Russian experience with FBRs for Japan's own program.

Japanese policy flies in the face of a strong international consensus among nuclear experts who are concerned about proliferation—a consensus that plutonium from dismantled weapons should be disposed of in one way or another and that Russian weapons plutonium should not be put to civilian use. Japan could take the lead in worldwide non-proliferation and denuclearization efforts by renouncing its own plutonium program and urging Russia to follow suit.

HEALTH AND
ENVIRONMENTAL RISKS

The stated goal of Japan's plutonium program is to establish "energy self-reliance" by breeding plutonium in FBRs. MOX burning in LWRs is only an intermediate step in preparing for the full commercialization of FBRs. Of course, plutonium itself is a very toxic substance. But what is most important from the standpoint of human health and the environment is that the effective utilization of plutonium as an energy source requires a difficult and complicated multifaceted fast-reactor nuclear-fuel cycle, entailing potentially hazardous environmental risks. No country has ever attempted such a program on a large scale.

A closed fast-breeder fuel cycle needs to incorporate the following processes:

(a) Reprocessing of LWR spent fuel;
(b) Processing and fabrication of extracted plutonium into MOX fuel;
(c) Burning of MOX fuel in FBRs;
(d) Reprocessing of FBR spent fuel;
(e) Repetition of steps b to d; and
(f) Transport of plutonium after each step if facility sites are located elsewhere.

If plutonium were to provide a significant percentage of the primary energy supply in Japan, the amount of plutonium to be handled and transported in the entire cycle would be as much as one hundred tons annually. In such a "plutonium economy," as many as fifty FBRs and three to four large-scale FBR reprocessing plants and MOX fabrication plants would be necessary to keep the whole cycle always active. This would pose an unprecedented threat to human beings and the environment and would generate huge amounts of radioactive waste.

Japan is often said to have a relatively good safety record in its past operation of light-water reactors, but in the case of light-water reactors, Japan has been able to profit from the experiences of LWR operations in the United States and other countries. This time, however, Japan will have to develop the whole LWR and FBR fuel cycle with little benefit from the experiences of other countries. Japan will face difficulties designing and developing the FBR technology on its own, particularly because, apart from the intrinsic technical difficulties of FBRs, the complicated and fine piping necessary for the sodium coolant of these reactors is generally considered to be very vulnerable to seismic shocks. The difficulties expected to be faced by Japan have already been observed in the prolonged construction and fuel fabrication processes of the Monju plant, which has been beset by technical problems and delays climaxed by the 1995 accident involving a sodium leak.

The transportation of separated plutonium also poses environmental and security risks and is particularly controversial in the case of Japanese plutonium separated in European reprocessing plants, since this plutonium has to be transported a long way from the reprocessing plant to the MOX fabrication plant in Europe and then all the way to Japan. The transportation of high-level radioactive waste (HLW) and other radioactive wastes[20] from Europe to Japan is also expected to be very cumbersome and controversial—and would meet with international opposition, as happened with the plutonium shipment on board the *Akatsuki-maru* in 1993.

Some experts assert that the reprocessing and fast-reactor fuel cycle would be preferable from the viewpoint of waste disposal because some of the waste could be burned as fuel. However, a lengthy process of repeated reprocessing, fuel fabrication, and burning would be necessary in order to substantially reduce the amount of undesirable long-lived waste elements. Moreover, new radioactive wastes would arise from this process. Consequently, this method is not realistic, nor would it be desirable in terms of its environmental impact.

THE ECONOMICS OF PLUTONIUM

The economic case for using plutonium fuel is extremely weak, whether plutonium is used as MOX for LWRs or for FBRs. According to the RAND report, there would be no economic advantage in utilizing plutonium fuel unless the spot price for processed uranium ore, known as yellow cake, rises to more than $100 per pound for MOX use in LWRs and $220 per pound in FBRs. Since the current spot price of yellow cake is well below $10 per pound, there is practically no prospect for plutonium fuel to have any commercial competitiveness in the foreseeable future. The RAND report predicts that plutonium will not become economically viable for at least fifty years in the case of MOX for LWRs and one hundred years in the case of MOX for FBRs.

Even this prediction should be regarded as optimistic, since the reprocessing cost in future reprocessing plants is expected to be much more expensive than was previously believed. The latest estimate[21] of the capital cost of the Rokkashomura reprocessing plant is 1,600 billion yen ($14.9 billion), which is five times as high as that for the British Thermal Oxide Reprocessing Plant and almost twice the current official estimate.

It is expected that it will take more than fifty years for a full-scale FBR fuel cycle to be commercialized and put in the hands of private enterprise. Thus, the government will have to keep investing heavily in the plutonium program for a long period of time, which will suppress research and development investment in alternative energy sources—such as renewable energy—and make Japan's energy policy less and less flexible. This trend is already evident in Japan (see figure 2-5).

The economic disadvantages of reliance on plutonium arouse concern in neighboring countries, since a heavy investment in plutonium without economic justification is regarded with good reason as being related to some hidden military ambition. I have actually heard many people in other Asian countries express their concern in this respect. The plutonium program lacks the economic justification necessary to relieve concerns regarding Japan's military intentions.

2-5. R&D for Energy (FY 1991)

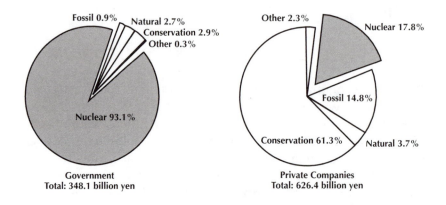

Fossil 0.9%
Natural 2.7%
Conservation 2.9%
Other 0.3%
Nuclear 93.1%

Government
Total: 348.1 billion yen

Other 2.3%
Nuclear 17.8%
Fossil 14.8%
Conservation 61.3%
Natural 3.7%

Private Companies
Total: 626.4 billion yen

Source: Science and Technology Yearbook, 1993.

ENERGY SECURITY?

Perhaps the most popular justification for a plutonium program that cannot be justified economically is that plutonium utilization could contribute to Japan's energy security. But plutonium cannot contribute significantly to Japan's energy supply throughout the next century due to the long doubling time of FBRs, regardless of the timing of the commercialization of FBRs. The so-called reactor doubling time, which is the time period required for the initial core plutonium load to be doubled, is estimated to be 40-45 years for Monju, and the inventory doubling time, which is the time period required for the total initial inventory in the fast-breeder fuel cycle to be doubled, is 80-100 years.[22] These figures cannot be improved much even with conceivable future fast-breeder designs. Since the doubling time is much longer than the expected life of fast-breeder reactors, breeding plutonium does not seem to be a workable strategy for Japan's energy security in the foreseeable future.

Moreover, in a plutonium-economy society that relies significantly on nuclear-weapons-usable material for energy, access to information essential to public safety and decision-making has to be restricted for security reasons. Nuclear facilities must be heavily protected against theft and sabotage. By its nature, a plutonium-economy society is not compatible with democracy.

Furthermore, even under strict information control and physical protection, the possibility of diversion cannot be ruled out. If tens of tons of plutonium are separated, transported, and used annually, it is hardly possible to keep the amount of material unaccounted for at what is a desirable level from the standpoint of preventing proliferation, due to the technical limitations of material accountancy.[23]

A FIVE-YEAR MORATORIUM

I believe that Japan should scrap its entire plutonium program. Japan has much more to gain than to lose by doing so. However, as a realistic approach that can be accepted by a wider range of people, I proposed a five-year moratorium on Japan's plutonium program at the JAEC's public hearing on the Long-Term Program for the Development and Utilization of Nuclear Energy, held March 4-5, 1994. A majority of those who spoke at the hearing expressed serious concern about Japan's current plutonium program, and my impression was that many well-informed prominent persons were supportive of a moratorium.

My proposal is to freeze for 5 years the operation of Monju, the construction of the Rokkashomura reprocessing plant, the reprocessing of Japanese spent fuel at the Tokai and European reprocessing plants, and the fabrication and utilization of MOX fuel for LWRs. I propose that, during the 5-year moratorium, a comprehensive environmental assessment of plutonium utilization be made—with the participation of a wide range of experts of differing opinions—and that the draft of the report be subjected to public review. The report should be finalized only after public discussion, which should contribute to decision-making on the long-term plutonium policy.

The assessment should include an examination of the following issues: safety, necessity, economics, nuclear proliferation, the societal impact of the plutonium economy, international relations, and alternatives to plutonium utilization. All of these issues need to be discussed on the basis of enhanced public access to information before the general public can decide about the wisdom of plutonium stockpiling and the utilization program, and now is the time for such a discussion. For the first time, the suspension of reprocessing will be an acceptable choice to utilities, because improved versions of a new technology for the long-term storage of spent fuel have now been developed. This technology, known as dry storage, requires less monitoring than storage in cooling ponds with its risk of corrosion. The Tokyo Electric Power Co. has already started dry storage at its Fukushima nuclear-power-plant site.

With the NPT extension conference successfully concluded, the momentum in favor of nuclear non-proliferation and denuclearization is growing, and civilian plutonium programs of all countries should be subject to international review in the context of an enhanced non-proliferation regime. A moratorium is also a wise and realistic choice for Japan in the context of the problems resulting from the dismantling of nuclear weapons. In both the United States and Russia, the political environment surrounding the disposition of weapons-grade plutonium is now in flux. At the same time, the development of new technology that could facilitate the disposition of surplus plutonium is progressing rapidly.

Instead of adding to the plutonium surplus, it is the international responsibility of Japan to focus on helping to reduce and contain the surplus while proceeding with a wide-ranging reassessment of its own plutonium program in which the Japanese public has full access to all of the facts necessary for a democratic decision.

NOTES

[1]A. Weinberg, "Revisiting the Second Nuclear Era: Probabilities and Practices," *Nuclear Engineering International*, November 1992, p. 36.

[2]Advisory Committee on Nuclear Fuel Recycling, Atomic Energy Commission, "Nuclear Fuel Recycling in Japan," August 1992.

[3]William J. Dircks, "Nuclear Fuel Recycling - The IAEA Perspective." Presentation at the 1992 Annual Meeting of the Japan Atomic Industry Forum, March 17, 1992.

[4]T. Sakata, "STA's Thinking," *Sekai*, November 1992, p. 81.

[5]Information made available by the STA to the Citizens' Nuclear Information Center concerning the throughput of the Tokai reprocessing plant in FY1992.

[6]J. Takagi, "Japanese Plutonium Utilization and Its Problems," Proceedings of the International Conference on Plutonium, 1991, p. 108.

[7]Committee on International Security and Arms Control, National Academy of Sciences, *Management and Disposition of Weapons Plutonium* (Washington: National Academy Press, 1994).

[8]W. A. Stauser, Chief, Weapons Branch, Division of Classification, Energy Research and Development Administration, letter to Richard Bowen, Division of International Security Affairs, August 4, 1977.

[9]B. G. Chow and K. A. Solomon, *Limiting the Spread of Weapon-Usable Fissile Materials* (Santa Monica: RAND Corporation, 1993).

10J. Carson Mark, "Explosive Properties of Reactor-Grade Plutonium," *Science & Global Security* (Los Angeles: Gordon and Breach Science Publishers, 1993), vol. 4, p. 1.

11R. Imai, "Review of New Mechanisms to Stem Nuclear Proliferation," *East Asia and Nuclear Proliferation*, Papers from the Twelfth Core Group Meeting of the Program for Presenting Nuclear Non-Proliferation, London, November 1992, p. 21.

12H. Kurihara, "A Japanese Perspective on Storage of Nuclear Material from Dismantled Warheads," Report on the International Workshop "Nuclear Disarmament and Non-Proliferation: Issues for International Action" Tokyo, March 1993, p. 4.

13"Plutonium Gap," *Asahi Shimbun*, November 29, 1992, p. 24.

14*Mainichi Shimbun*, August 1, 1994, p. 1.

15*Asahi Shimbun*, February 7, 1994, p. 3.

16*Nihow Keizai*, March 12, 1995, p. 3.

17*Nuclear Fuel*, October 10, 1994, p. 15.

18V. N. Mikhailov, "Plutonium in Nuclear Power Industry," presented to the Roundtable on the Current Issues on Plutonium, Tokyo, February 1994.

19S. Sakata, "A Personal View on Future Options of Plutonium Recovered from Nuclear Weapons," Report on the International Workshop "Nuclear Disarmament and Non-Proliferation: Issues for International Action," Tokyo, March 1993.

20All forms of radioactive waste resulting from the reprocessing of Japanese spent fuel in Europe should be sent back to Japan in principle, in accordance with reprocessing contracts between Japanese utilities and European reprocessors. French law for radioactive-waste management stipulates that all radioactive wastes of foreign origin should be sent back after a minimum storage period. However, there is much talk about returning only HLW, substituting it for intermediate- and low-level wastes (radiological-toxicity-equivalent substitution). Indeed, there is still no plan in Japan to build facilities for the storage or disposal of low- and intermediate-level wastes from Europe.

21*Denryoku Jiji Tsushin* (Electric Power Topics Newsletter), No. 4177, January 24, 1994.

22J. Takagi, Commentary to Japanese edition of *Plutonium, Deadly Gold of Nuclear Age*, International Physicians for the Prevention of Nuclear War and the Institute for Energy and Environmental Research 1993, Japanese edition (Tokyo: Diamond Ltd., 1993), p.32.

23M. Miller, "Are IAEA Safeguards on Plutonium Bulk-handling Facilities Effective?" (Washington: Nuclear Control Institute, 1990), p. 10.

CHAPTER 3

JAPANESE AMBITIONS, U.S. CONSTRAINTS, AND SOUTH KOREA'S NUCLEAR FUTURE

TAEWOO KIM

THE FOCUS ON JAPAN

Despite the Agreed Framework concluded between the United States and the Democratic People's Republic of Korea on October 21, 1994, the question of whether or not North Korea has already built the bomb remains unanswered. President Bill Clinton declared in 1993 that "North Korea cannot be allowed to develop a nuclear bomb." But the Agreed Framework allowed Pyongyang to maintain its nuclear devices—bombs-in-the-basement, bombs ready to be assembled, hidden plutonium, or whatever—by delaying special inspection by several years.[1]

This is why some South Korean nuclear specialists, including this author, believe that U.S. policy may have switched from "prevent a North Korean bomb" to "cover up the North Korean bomb." Moreover, a structural dilemma results from the nature of the U.S.–bestowed "denuclearization of the Korean peninsula" policy. Should North Korea defy the policy, South Korea will be the only non-nuclear state in the region barred from the full development of even the peaceful use of nuclear power while nevertheless facing the North Korean nuclear capability and the nuclear weapons of neighboring states. On the other hand, if the policy is successful, the Korean peninsula alone will be a non-nuclear enclave surrounded by nuclear or near-nuclear powers—such as Japan—all of whom have invaded the Korean peninsula in one way or another.

On top of this dilemma, South Korea has no reason to expect much from its neighbors with regard to a solution of the North Korean nuclear problem. China may welcome a measure of ambiguity with respect to the North's capability as diplomatic leverage vis-à-vis the United States, while Japan has even more reason to welcome the status quo. A confrontational division of the Korean peninsula offers neighboring powers enormous leverage via-à-vis the two Koreas. Furthermore, Japan, with its gigantic economic and technological power, accounting for roughly 15 percent of the world's gross national product (GNP), will easily be able to counter any North Korean threat if it decides to do so. Not surprisingly, some South Korean analysts believe that Japanese leaders may in the future utilize the potential threat from North Korea as an excuse to modernize Japan's missile forces or to acquire a nuclear-weapons capability.[2] Neither is it surprising that many Asian countries— including South Korea, which is still haunted by the nightmare of Japanese colonial militarism only five decades ago—fret over the question: "Will Japan remain an economic power but shackled to second-class status in the new world order, or will it become a true superpower with corresponding military might?"

This is why Japan's defense policy in general, and its nuclear policy in particular, has become a topic of keen interest to South Korea. I will devote much of this essay to assessing Japan's defense posture—predicting how Japan's National Defense Program Outline is likely to be implemented and explaining why Japan's nuclear policy is regarded with suspicion by its neighbors. I will then underline the contrast between Japan's development of its nuclear option with the blessing of the United States, and South Korea's inability to develop reprocessing facilities for peaceful purposes as a result of the manner in which Seoul and Washington have dealt with the North Korean nuclear threat. Finally, I will suggest a new nuclear policy for Japan, one that will be conducive to reducing the nuclear instability on and around the peninsula and thus to establishing a nuclear-free Korea. For the region as a whole, it would be healthier if Japan would shepherd a responsible multilateral arrangement toward the peaceful development of a shared atomic industry instead of flaunting its own technological and economic edge. In a nuclear world, that edge is a worrisome matter for its neighbors.

THE FUTURE OF JAPANESE DEFENSE POLICY

T wo different perspectives stand out in the current debate on the future direction of Japan's defense policy: a traditional pacifist view, which predicts that Japan will continue to adopt a minimalist approach and will thus become one of the rare examples of a state that wields gigantic economic and technological power without corresponding military might; and a revisionist Hobbesian view, which expects that Japan will inevitably unsheathe its sword once again. Taifu Yu, for example, contends that the end of the Cold War has created a political environment that renders any substantial increase in defense spending simply less possible than before.[3] He goes on to argue that Japan, with the help of the United States, should participate in disarmament talks with Russia and help initiate the dismantling of the Cold War structure in Asia. Likewise, Thomas U. Berger argues that Japan's imbedded anti-militarism will not allow it to rearm.[4]

In contrast, many "realist" theorists predict that Japan, with its enormous economic and technological prowess, will seek a greater military role both regionally and globally. In this regard, Berger points out, the classical realists, who assume that nations always seek to maximize their power, including their military might, and the structural realists, who hold that nations want to expand their power only insofar as needed for security from perceived external threats,[5] do not differ in that they both expect Japan to rearm.

Interestingly, a third party of theorists, such as Peter J. Katzenstein and Nobuo Okawara, argue that both the pessimistic and the optimistic perspectives are mistaken because Japan's foreign policy choices are determined not by international variables but by the domestic normative context. They point to the fact that economic security is an uncontested norm in Japan while military security is deeply contested, and that civilian supremacy over the military is firmly entrenched. For these reasons, they say, Japan will not pursue a status as a military power.[6]

For this author, all three perspectives are partially valid, since Japan's defense policy will be affected simultaneously by retarding variables and by catalysts that facilitate rearmament, both of which abound in number and variety.

Retarding variables, now and for the future, include the still-robust Japan–U.S. partnership; the end of the Cold War; the waning Russian threat and the non-confrontational Russian navy; possible progress in regional arms control; the emergence of a multinational security framework in Asia; unmitigated suspicion on the part of Japan's neighboring states; domestic Japanese support for economic over military security; Japanese anti-militarist, anti-nuclear sentiment; and the pervasively democratic and pluralistic domestic system. Facilitating variables include the lingering Hobbesian nature of international politics; the still-valid logic of "realist" doctrine; the trade frictions and naval competition with the United States; the revival of Japanese nationalism and support for a Pax Nipponica; the possibility that North Korea possesses nuclear weapons; the Defense Agency's resistance to arms reductions; the emergence of worldwide resource nationalism; China's military modernization and a possible Japan-China power struggle over regional hegemony; and the potential disintegration of China with its inevitably disrupting effects.

Due to the existence of these variables, any prediction of a sharp, rapid change based on a specific set of variables could be dangerously misleading. George Friedman and Meredith Lebard may be exaggerating when they contend that a showdown between the United States and Japan over control of the sea lanes (for resource security) will be unavoidable.[7] Likewise, Katzenstein and Okawara may be oversimplifying when they argue that Japan's security policy is shaped largely by domestic rather than international determinants. Many Japanese authors are committing a similar mistake of oversimplification when they focus solely on the defense aspects of their current and potential military capabilities and their own military vulnerabilities.[8]

FROM THE "FREE RIDE" TO "WAR LIQUIDATION"

My own interim conclusion is that the changes in Japan's defense policy, if any, will be incremental and gradual. As Katzenstein and Okawara observe, Japan's domestic normative framework may not permit sudden variations in defense policy, despite outside changes.

Realist interpretations also suggest the likelihood of gradual change, since the geopolitical environment surrounding Japan will make it take a prudent attitude toward shifting its policy line. This will be so particularly because Japan is in the center of a quadrilateral power balance in the Pacific that is unique geographically in that the four largest powers lie in close proximity.

Before seeking to project future trends, it is necessary to review the evolution of Japan's defense policy in recent decades. This evolution can be classified into three phases. First, the postwar period, to the end of 1970, could be termed a "free ride" phase, when Japan depended completely on the U.S.–Japan alliance system for security. This period ended after Yasuhiro Nakasone became minister of the Self-Defense Agency in 1970 and the Nixon Doctrine dictated the non-involvement of American ground forces. The second phase, from 1970 to 1990, was an "expansion" period when a mix of economic revitalization and other indigenous factors led to Japan's expansion of its defense perimeter throughout its territory, the surrounding territorial waters, and a 1,000-mile radius of sea lanes of communication. Under the Nakasone cabinet, in particular, several external factors, such as the Soviet threat and U.S. demands for greater burden-sharing, have all pushed Japan to consume the world's third largest defense budget (after the United States and Russia).

The third phase began in 1990, when the death of Emperor Hirohito and a more flexible interpretation of Japan's Constitution signaled the advent of the "war liquidation period." The dispatch of minesweepers to the Gulf War, passage of the U.N. Peacekeeping Operations (PKO) Cooperation Bill in 1992, and the dispatch of peacekeepers to Cambodia reflected this new flexibility, prompting fears in both Japan and neighboring countries that dominant elements in Japan want to pave the way for a future role as "world gendarme." Though the 1990 New Mid-Term Defense Program was modified in 1992, reflecting the dissipating Cold War and the worldwide arms-control mood, the plan to purchase high-tech weapons, including multiple-launch rocket systems (MLRS), Airborne Early Warning/Ground Integration Segment (AEGIS) ships, and Airborne Warning and Control (AWAC) aircraft, was kept intact.

Of course different interpretations are possible. Berger, for example, interprets Japan's defense spending during the 1970s and 1980s quite differently: "Japan's military buildup took place in close consultation with the U.S. to complement the U.S. forces in the region, with a heavy emphasis on defensive weapons and little independent capacity for power projection."[9] Similarly, Katzenstein and Okawara hold that the PKO bill did not violate Article 9 of the Constitution, since it authorized only non-combat peacekeeping and humanitarian activities.[10] Berger argues that Japan, by sending the minesweepers grudgingly only after hostilities had ceased, demonstrated its reluctance to expand its military role.[11]

Nevertheless, it is undeniable that, for the first time, Japan sent its forces overseas, breaking the old taboo, and that pressures are growing for removal of the ban in the 1992 PKO bill on participation in peacekeeping activities that could involve a combat role. To some Asian countries, Berger's emphasis on the defensive nature of Japan's weapons systems seems irresponsible, particularly because it is increasingly difficult to distinguish offensive from defensive weapons. Why Japan's acquisition of high-tech military technologies and sophisticated weapons systems does not give it an "independent" military capability is not at all clear.

THE GROWTH OF DEFENSE SPENDING

What is conspicuous in the trend of Japan's defense policy is the relentless, albeit incremental, growth in the sophistication of its military capability. What is meaningful is the consistent growth of defense spending, which reached 4,700 billion yen (or $43.92 billion at the April 1996 average exchange rate of 107 yen per dollar)[12] in fiscal 1995, paralleling Japanese economic growth. This is more important than whether or not Japan's defense budget remains within the 1 percent stricture first announced by Prime Minister Takeo Miki in 1976 and removed by Nakasone in 1987. The Defense Agency's assurances that Japan possesses only "a minimum basic defensive power" and other declaratory diplomatic language about the nature of the Japanese military forces should not blind us to the growing sophistication of Japanese weaponry.

Likewise, the sheer size of Japan's armed forces—234,000 men, 1,200 tanks, 150 F-15 fighters, 17 submarines, etc.—may not be as meaningful as Japan's overall potential to mobilize and its manufacturing capability for military purposes. Japan is now co-developing F-16 fighters with the United States and is building the formidable AEGIS ships, even though their off-the-shelf purchase would be much less expensive. Whether intended or not, Japan's steady progression from the "free-riding" and "expansion and Japanization" phases into the "postwar-liquidation" era enables one to predict a continuation of the gradual yet impressive growth in Japan's military capability, regardless of the official language.

It is not surprising that Japanese leaders believe their nation should continue to increase its indigenous defense production base and modernize its military to be prepared to cope with a treacherous world. Japan faces a dangerous international environment: a multipolar world in which Japan, as a pole, needs equidistant diplomacy with other powers; the weakening of the Japan(U.S. alliance and vehement trade disputes; the inevitability of a power struggle with China; the formidable Russian navy; and the enhanced nuclear threat from Russia, China, and even North Korea. A fourth phase of defense policy for Japan, in which it openly pursues military power, including a nuclear capability corresponding to its economic and technological power, may become unavoidable.

The end of the Cold War and the reduction in the Russian threat have not altered the trend of incremental growth coupled with a growing sophistication in weaponry. Despite the modifications of the National Defense Program Outline in 1992 and 1995 to reduce the purchase of weapons, Japan has only marginally scaled down its plans to purchase high-tech weapons needed for a long-distance force projection combat capability, including MLRS rockets, AEGIS ships, SSM-1 missiles, and AWAC aircraft. Significantly, it has established an integrated intelligence headquarters like the U.S. CIA, and it has purchased military intelligence satellites and E-767 AWACs. Special attention should be paid to Japan's demonstrated capability to develop intercontinental missiles and to its current consideration of a theater missile defense system. The successful launch of the Japanese-made H-2 rocket on February 4, 1994, was accompanied by assurances that the rocket will be used solely for peaceful purposes. But it clearly gives Japan a capability for developing an intercontinental ballistic missile overnight. This capability should be viewed against the background of the steady progress in Japan's nuclear-power program and the danger that it may serve as the basis for a nuclear-weapons program.

JAPANESE NUCLEAR POLICY: THE RECORD

With its forty-seven commercial reactors, Japan is the third largest generator of nuclear power in the world. As is the case in many countries, Japan's atomic industry has its own special characteristics, of which four stand out. A close analysis will easily reveal, among other things, a surprising consistency in Japanese nuclear policy-making and a tenacity in pursuit of indigenous and top-quality technologies.

JAPANIZATION

Since 1956, the Japanese Atomic Energy Commission (JAEC) and the Science and Technology Agency have regularly announced Long-Term Programs for the Development and Utilization of Nuclear Energy; the eighth of these programs was issued in 1992. In addition, the Ministry of International Trade and Industry (MITI) has been issuing "energy demand forecasts and conservation plans" between the Long-Term Programs, thus justifying any need to revise them if necessary. For example, in 1990, MITI announced that the nation's energy consumption was moving ahead of its GNP growth rates. On that basis, the JAEC announced in 1991 a schedule for the completion of the fuel cycle that would include consumption of a massive amount of plutonium by 2010, which provided the rationale for the ambitious and comprehensive Long-Term Program of 1992. Through the eight Long-Term Programs for the Development and Utilization of Nuclear Energy issued since 1956, Japan has consistently taken every step necessary in pursuit of maximum autonomy in all aspects of nuclear-power generation (see table 3-1).

Japan has succeeded brilliantly in the phased development of its atomic industry: from the nuclear dark ages of the 1940s, when all atomic activities were prohibited; through the 1950s, when it paved the way for its nuclear industry by institutionalizing legal arrangements and basic research systems; to the 1960s, when Japan acquired a technological base, to the 1970s and 1980s, when it secured and commercialized key nuclear technologies. Japan is one of the few countries to enter the twenty-first century with such a potential in fusion, fast-breeder reactors (FBRs), and laser enrichment. It began building a large-scale reprocessing plant in 1993 in Rokkashomura; the plant is scheduled to be operational by the year

2000, with a capacity of 800 tons per year. A storage engineering center will be built at Horonobe on Hokkaido for high-tech radioactive waste storage and for research and development on geological disposal technology. Japan will remain one of the few countries that spends such an enormous amount of money for atomic research and development—218.2 billion yen ($2.03 billion) for 1993.[13] In sum, Japan's effort to indigenize the entire gamut of nuclear technologies is impressive by any standard.

THE PLUTONIUM SURPLUS

The scope and character of the Japanese atomic industry defy most international trends. A certain portion of its atomic capability is hardly justifiable economically, and the political impact of the Japanese nuclear program is profoundly destabilizing . Japan is seeking to manufacture indigenously every aspect of a nuclear power plant. Even the Japanese nuclear-power community is concerned about financial viability, overcapacity, and the necessity of maintaining technological excellence.[14] The amount of plutonium Japan intends to store creates a growing apprehension at home and abroad, particularly when a global oversupply of this dangerous substance is imminent due to the scheduled dismantling of American and Russian nuclear warheads.

Although Japan has repeatedly emphasized its peaceful intentions for plutonium consumption by making public its plan to use large volumes of plutonium for FBRs and plutonium-and-uranium mixed oxide (MOX) fuel development, the sheer amount of plutonium Japan plans to secure, as well as the possible surplus therefrom, is a source of legitimate concern on the part of the neighboring Asian countries, including South Korea. Tables 3-2 and 3-3 show the comparison between Japan's announced amount of plutonium in storage and its projected consumption, as estimated by the Korean Institute for Defense Analyses (KIDA) Nuclear Study Group under my direction.[15]

According to these estimates, Japan will have some thirteen tons of surplus plutonium in storage by the year 2004. An additional 2.6 tons could be saved if construction of the Taigan advanced thermal reactor were to be delayed. Estimates and reports of possible modifications of course differ. According to the plutonium user plans issued by the JAEC in August 1991, for example, Japan is to secure some 85 tons of plutonium, while its aggregate consumption

3-1. Japanese Long-Term Programs for the Development and Utilization of Nuclear Energy

1st Program (1956–1960)
Prepared ground for development of atomic industry.
Introduced foreign technology for indigenous power-reactor construction.
Selected fast-breeder reactor (FBR) as final goal.
Initiated training and education of nuclear scientists.
Established plan to develop atomic-propelled ships.
Established plan to acquire fusion technology.
Enacted Atomic Energy Basic Law.
Established Japan Atomic Energy Research Institute.
Established twenty-year nuclear-power-supply plan.
Purchased a gas-cooled reactor from Britain.
Decided to acquire reprocessing technology and facilities and to develop indigenous FBRs.
Acquired high-level safety technologies for reactors and other nuclear facilities.

2nd Program (1961–1966)
Transfered technologies nearing commercial use to private sector for further research and development (R&D); government continued to implement R&D for other technologies needing further funds.
Acquired technologies for atomic-propelled ships.
Drastically diversified the application of atomic technologies to other industries.
Established the Power Reactor and Nuclear Fuel Development Corporation (PNC).
Set up a plan for Japanization of fuel cycle.
Decided upon LWRs as the main reactor type for commercial power generation.

3rd Program (1967–1971)
Acquired contracts for development of overseas uranium mines and imports.
LWRs decided upon as main reactor type for commercial power generation.
Established a national-level research project for acquisition of complete fusion technology.
Dramatically increased nuclear-power-generation goals.

4th Program (1956–1960)

Acquired indigenous safety system.

Secured international network for nuclear fuel supply.

Succeeded in developing local enrichment technologies and began construction of an enrichment plant.

Constructed a reprocessing plant in Tokai.

Test-operated Joyo FBR.

Reduced nuclear-power-generation goals.

Implemented national-level research projects for "LWR to FBR" and "FBR to Fusion Reactor" transition.

5th Program (1978–1981)

Standardized and improved LWRs.

Developed indigenous downstream fuel-cycle.

Greatly strengthened its international competitive edge.

Reduced nuclear-power-generation goals.

6th Program (1982–1986)

Set up plan to develop completely indigenous fuel cycle.

Sharply increased budget allocation for R&D, fuel-cycle construction, fusion, etc.

Constructed an atomic complex in Rokkashomura.

Completed comprehensive plans for treatment of enriched uranium, spent fuel, low-radiation wastes, etc.

7th Program (1987–1991)

Intensified R&D function of PNC.

Set 2020 as goal year for commercialization of Monju FBR.

Set plans for development of future (untapped) nuclear technologies.

Operated Monju FBR.

Completed various nuclear/environmental technologies.

8th Program (1992–1997)

Expanded international technological cooperation, particularly with Russia and several East European countries.

Established comprehensive plan for full-fledged utilization of plutonium.

Revised Japan–U.S. atomic cooperation agreement, thus increasing Japanese independence in plutonium storage.

3-2.   Sources and Amounts of Japanese Plutonium (tons)

Source	Period		
	1978–1990	1991–1992	1993–2004
Tokai Reprocessing Plant	2.75	3.28	7.02
Rokkashomura Reprocessing Plant	-	-	29.40
Reprocessing Contracts in U.K. and France	1.33	1.33	26.15
Totals	4.08	4.61	62.57

3-3.   Estimated Plutonium Consumption and Amounts (tons)

Consumer	Period		
	1978–1990	1991–1992	1993–2004
Joyo FBR	2.45	1.09	0.84
Fugen FBR	-	1.08	0.90
Monju FBR	-	1.00	4.32
Daigan FBR	-	-	2.60
MOX for LWRs	-	0.90	41.10
Totals	2.45	4.07	49.76

will be from 82 to 93 tons. However, the consumption total may prove to be lower—thus leaving an even larger surplus—and there are other ways in which Japan could set aside plutonium. A JAEC *White Paper* published in 1994, which states that Japan had 10.94 tons of plutonium at home and abroad, validates the estimate of the KIDA Nuclear Study Group.

What is equally noteworthy is that Japan's plutonium plan is not compatible with worldwide trends in dealing with surplus plutonium. The two sources that contribute the most to an oversupply of sensitive nuclear material—highly enriched uranium (HEU) and plutonium— are the dismantling of the American and Russian nuclear warheads and the increasing inevitability of spent fuel reprocessing. Today many countries are storing hundreds of tons of spent fuel. The aggregate amount predicted to be possessed by the member countries of the Organisation for Economic Co-operation and Development is now estimated at over 180,000 tons. It is only common sense to grapple with how to treat the high-level radioactive spent fuel.

It is imperative to find effective ways to treat the increasing amount of spent fuel and to consume peacefully the new resources therefrom. According to the 1991 Strategic Arms Reduction Treaty (START II), the two nuclear superpowers will dismantle some 15,000 strategic warheads, leaving fewer than 10,000 intact. Considerable amounts of HEU and plutonium will thus be extracted. The amounts will snowball when combined with the weapons-grade material that has been earmarked for future weapons use: some 1,700 tons of HEU and 285 tons of plutonium.[16]

This enormous surplus will create a variety of costly storage and management problems, particularly for poverty-stricken Russia. For this reason, the Russian Ministry of Atomic Energy agreed to sell 500 tons of HEU annually to Allied Signal Corporation of the United States. Unlike enriched uranium, which can be diluted for commercial use, plutonium must be consumed peacefully as is. Thus Russia wants buyers from Japan, where there are FBRs, impressive MOX projects, and other plutonium-consuming projects. The "Russian connection" will increasingly become an imperative for Japan.

An inescapable interim conclusion is that since it is very important to consume surplus plutonium peacefully in order to help retard nuclear weapons proliferation, Japan should focus on finding ways to consume peacefully the $260 billion worth of plutonium[17] to be extracted from nuclear warheads instead of engaging in excessive

3-4. Existing Highly Enriched Uranium Stocks (tons)

Status	United States	Russia	Total
in warheads	500	600	1,000
in storage	–	600	600
Total	**500**	**1,200**	**1,700**

3-5. Existing Plutonium Stocks (tons)

Status	United States	Russia	Total
in warheads	100	95	195
in storage	90	–	90
Total	**190**	**95**	**285**

plutonium storage on Japanese soil. This would be lucrative while at the same time contributing to non-proliferation goals.

MILITARY POTENTIAL

The Japanese atomic industry has definitely acquired a military potential, whether intentionally or not. Consider the fact that plutonium is the element most directly usable for weapons production and that 5-10 kilograms of plutonium is enough to forge a single 20-kiloton nuclear warhead. The aforementioned 13 tons of plutonium could be used to make well over a thousand Hiroshima-size bombs if Japan were to withdraw from the Treaty on the Non-Proliferation of Nuclear Weapons. Given Japan's highly developed electrical, electronic, and aerospace industries, it is one of the few countries that could be armed with superb nuclear forces and superior command and control systems.

Japan's impending laser-enrichment technology deserves particular attention. Laser technology, in which Japan is by far the frontrunner, makes it possible to produce weapons-grade 90 percent–enriched uranium very quickly in a very small plant. This contrasts starkly with both the conventional gas-diffusion method, which requires 3,000 steps to extract weapons-grade uranium, and the thirty-step centrifugal method.

Although Japan's atomic industry is subject to international monitoring and has been dedicated to strictly peaceful purposes, the objective fact that the nation's nuclear industry has ample military potential is a burden to neighboring countries in this Hobbesian world. Consequence-centered analysts can argue with justification that Japanese nuclear policy has been implemented under what George Quester calls an "asymptomatic strategy."[18]

THE ROLE OF LEADERS

Suspicions concerning the military potential of Japan's nuclear program are underlined by the fact that it has been promoted from the outset by a declared advocate of a Japanese nuclear-weapons capability: Yasuhiro Nakasone.

In 1945, Nakasone, then a young navy lieutenant, personally witnessed the Hiroshima and Nagasaki bombings. After the war, he became the youngest member of the Japanese Diet, and in 1951 he played a primary role in preventing the 1951 U.S.–Japan San

Francisco Peace Treaty from prohibiting the development of a Japanese atomic industry. In 1954, when the Japanese Diet allocated a symbolic amount to the first atomic budget, Nakasone played a key role. It was also Nakasone who, in 1956, first suggested the construction of three power reactors and, in 1966, initiated a plan for self-sufficiency in FBR and reprocessing technologies. As the Director of the Science and Technology Agency, Nakasone presided over the enactment of the Atomic Energy Basic Law, which committed the country to a plan for nuclear development that has received budgetary support from the Diet ever since. It was in 1970, when Nakasone was its Director, that the Japanese Defense Agency published its *White Paper* indicating that the possession of "defensive" nuclear weapons would not be unconstitutional.[19] It was Prime Minister Nakasone who, in the early 1980s, shaped a consensus within the bureaucracy and the governing Liberal Democratic Party that Japan should insist on a relaxation of the tight controls in its nuclear cooperation agreement with the United States when the accord came up for renewal in 1988. Under the revised "Agreement for Cooperation Concerning the Peaceful Use of Nuclear Energy," which was negotiated with the Reagan Administration in 1988, Japan acquired the freedom to store plutonium on its own soil. The previous obligation to gain U.S. approval batch-by-batch for the right to reprocess U.S.–origin uranium fuel and to use the resulting plutonium was replaced by a thirty-year advance consent clause that gave Japan the authority to bring back the plutonium extracted from Japanese spent fuel reprocessed in Europe.[20]

While Nakasone is the most outspoken advocate of a Japanese nuclear-weapons capability, all of the other Japanese leaders who have preceded and followed him as Prime Minister have also supported the development of an autonomous nuclear-fuel cycle.

As early as 1959, under Prime Minister Nobosuke Kishi, Japan had already separated plutonium. Prime Minister Eisaku Sato pushed through the second Long-Term Program for the Development and Utilization of Nuclear Energy in 1964, which led to the construction of a 210-ton annual capacity reprocessing plant in Tokai (completed in 1977). Initially reversing the Reagan policy, the Carter Administration forbade operation of the Tokai plant, but Prime Ministers Takeo Fukuda and Masayoshi Ohira, after a long negotiation with the United States, finally succeeded in gaining approval for partial operation of the plant on the condition that it would reprocess no more than 99 tons for the initial two years and that Japan would not take any steps to build a second reprocessing plant. Later, however, Prime Minister Zenko Suzuki talked President Ronald Reagan into a 1981 joint declaration that allowed Japan to operate the Tokai plant without restrictions by 1984, and to construct a second reprocessing facility. By the time Tokai became fully operational in 1988, the Japanese reprocessing endeavor had been in progress for almost thirty years. When the Rokkashomura reprocessing plant is completed in the year 2000, Japan will have the world's third largest commercial reprocessing capacity,[21] next only to the United States (2,100 tons) and France (1,200 tons).

In addition to its plutonium program, Japan acquired enriched uranium by centrifugal separation as early as 1966 and later constructed a pilot enrichment plant in Ninyotoke. Another enrichment plant in Rokkashomura, which became operational in 1984, with an annual capacity of 150 tons per year, is being enlarged to a 600-ton capacity and is slated for eventual further expansion to a 1,500-ton capacity.

All told, the impressive array of nuclear facilities in operation or near completion in Japan includes 47 power reactors, 15 research reactors, 2 experimental FBRs, 2 ATRs, 9 critical facilities, 5 reprocessing facilities (including 3 of experimental size), 5 enrichment facilities, and 10 large-scale research compounds, among others. This achievement would have been impossible without the farsighted commitment of Japanese leaders. Japan is now the frontrunner in many areas of nuclear development, notably fast-breeder and nuclear-fusion technology, and appears likely to become the front-runner in the commercial utilization of MOX fuel as well.

SOUTH KOREA'S NUCLEAR DILEMMA

Contrast Japan's systematic development of its nuclear option with South Korea's plight as a non-nuclear enclave surrounded by nuclear or near-nuclear powers. President Roh Tae Woo's decision to sign a denuclearization agreement with North Korea in December, 1991, went far beyond what was necessary to achieve South Korean security against the danger of a North Korean nuclear-weapons capability.

The 1991 North Korea–South Korea agreement is in reality two agreements: one renouncing possession of nuclear weapons and committing itself to the peaceful use of atomic power, and the other renouncing possession of enrichment and reprocessing facilities. Ironically, this division into two parts is both logical and paradoxical: logical in that enrichment and reprocessing can be misused in nuclear-weapons manufacturing, and paradoxical in that the enrichment and reprocessing are intrinsically peaceful technologies that South Korea needs very much to maximize the benefits of the peaceful uses of atomic energy. A kitchen knife, though a lethal weapon in some circumstances, is not a weapon in the hands of law-abiding citizens. This is why some experts, including this author, have frankly criticized the second part of the agreement, which prohibits the core technologies needed for a peaceful atomic industry.

To be blunt, the second part of the agreement reflected the global non-proliferation objectives of the United States and the pressures on South Korea as a U.S. ally. It would not have been adopted voluntarily by Seoul as a necessary step to extinguish the nuclear threat from Pyongyang. It should be remembered that President Park Chung-Hee's attempt in the mid-1970s to acquire a reprocessing facility was blocked by the United States. Since then, the fear of the North Korean nuclear problem has effectively prevented any similar attempts. The South Korean government asserts that "the renunciation of enrichment and reprocessing facilities was inevitable so that South Korea could legitimately demand that North Korea discard the Yongbyon reprocessing plant." Yet this position rests on faulty logic. The truth is that once nuclear facilities are open and subject to IAEA inspection, they can hardly be abused secretly for military purposes. Therefore, the Yongbyon plant ceased to be a threat from the moment it became subject to international inspection. On the other hand, even should the Yongbyon plant be dismantled, the spent fuel it produced prior to inspection, and that which other clandestine facilities produce, will still constitute a threat. The nuclear threat from a safeguarded country comes from hidden facilities or the secret storage of plutonium. Thus it would have been enough that Seoul demand faithful inspection of the plant. Safeguarding the Yongbyon facility would have provided ample justification for South Korea's possession of a reprocessing plant, which it needs very badly for its own atomic industry.

It is no exaggeration to say that the future of oil-deficient South

Korea hinges on the maximum use of nuclear energy, and that the South's lack of enrichment and reprocessing facilities is a missing link that undermines the nation's energy and technology security.

South Korea currently operates nine power reactors and ranks tenth in the world in nuclear energy production, with a total capacity of 7,620,000 kilowatts. Of South Korea's 1991 total electricity output, nuclear power accounted for 49.1 percent.

Since eight of South Korea's nine commercial reactors are light-water reactors using enriched uranium as fuel, South Korea with no enrichment facilities continues to import enriched uranium from foreign countries. Only the Wolsung No. 1 plant is a Canadian heavy-water reactor that can use unenriched uranium directly.

Among the numerous benefits of reprocessing technology, at least four stand out:

First, the most valuable type of isotope, known as the trans-uranic radioisotope (TRU), can only be produced through reprocessing. TRUs are an important source of heat generation and can be used for important medical purposes, such as cancer treatment, as well as for a variety of industrial and agricultural processes. Without reprocessing facilities, South Korea has been importing TRUs from abroad, thus limiting their use. The TRU isotopes include neptunium and americium. Neptunium can be recycled into nuclear fuel, and americium can be used to make alpha-ray sensors and as a source of fuel for subminiature reactors for satellites. While research in these fields is going on in technologically advanced countries, South Korea is destined to fall behind in the years to come.

Second, reprocessing is an important part of spent fuel treatment. In the absence of reprocessing, hundreds of tons of spent fuel must be kept submerged at great cost in a storage pool, awaiting the day when it can be put to use as a valuable resource.

Third, as long as it is used for peaceful purposes, the plutonium extracted through reprocessing becomes an indispensable asset for the future. A maximum of 10 kilograms of plutonium can be extracted when one ton of nuclear spent fuel is reprocessed. Some 2.5 tons of plutonium could be extracted from the 237 tons of spent fuel produced in South Korea annually. The Uljin Unit-1 reactor alone can produce about 270 kilograms per year.

Separated plutonium is used as a fuel for fast-breeder reactors. As Japan has recognized, the breeder reactor is a magic lantern that produces new plutonium while using plutonium and uranium as fuel. It is the state-of-the-art, resource-recycling technology, and it can stretch the life span of uranium about 60 times over usage in light-water reactors. In addition, plutonium can be mixed into unenriched uranium to produce a type of fuel known as mixed oxide (MOX) fuel, which can be used in ordinary reactors. In the short term, reprocessing is less economical than importing enriched uranium, but it is an indispensable technology for South Korea. Despite its economic inefficiency, the importance of MOX fuel in terms of energy security is likely to increase.

Fourth, reprocessing serves as a nuclear-waste-treatment technology. The spent fuel contains plutonium, uranium, krypton, xenon, iodine, and many other nuclear fissionables. One ton of spent fuel, high-radioactive nuclear material produces 0.1 cubic meters of high-radioactive nuclear waste that can be compressed or solidified, neutralized, and permanently discarded. To a peaceful user reprocessing separates resources from waste and offers both resource recycling and permanent waste disposal.

Unlike North Korea, which does not have commercial light-water reactors, necessitating fuel recycling, energy-poor South Korea—with its nine commercial reactors in operation and nine more to be built by 2006—is in dire need of both technologies.

CONCLUSION:
A NUCLEAR-FREE EAST ASIA

The moderate but consistent expansion of Japan's nuclear capability has increasingly aroused misgivings on the part of its neighbors. At one time, neighboring countries hoped that the United States would impose restraints on Japan. But given Japan's growing interest in nuclear technologies and its defense policy as a whole, it is highly unlikely that the Clinton Administration's new non-proliferation policy, which places emphasis on *protection against* rather than *prevention of* proliferation and on the suppression of the plutonium cycle,[22] will retard Japan's atomic development programs significantly.

It is not my intention to suggest that the Japanese atomic industry is a "wolf in sheep's clothing." But it is clear that for a nuclear-capable country such as Japan, if the completion of technological

105

means is a "necessary pre-condition" for nuclearization, then a certain global politico-military climate combined with a rise in internal nationalism could provide a "sufficient" condition. Japan should recognize that such a possibility is eminently plausible to its neighbors. Accordingly, with its increasing responsibility for the stability of Northeast Asia, Japan should pay greater attention to the geopolitical, psychological, and diplomatic impact of a unilaterally ambitious nuclear policy. If Japan's nuclear policy were reshaped and moderated with an eye to the concerns of its neighbors, then prospects for the establishment of a nuclear weapons–free Korea, and thus for a more stable Northeast Asia, would be greatly improved.

The nuclear powers and Japan have to realize that neither South Korea nor North Korea will remain content with the current concept of a nuclear-free Korea, which not only subjects the peninsula to the potential nuclear threats posed by surrounding countries but also unjustifiably restricts the peaceful use of nuclear energy. This is why the concept of a nuclear-free East Asia[23] should be further developed as an international regime satisfying at least five conditions:

(1) It should cover the eastern area of China and Russia as well as the Korean peninsula, Taiwan, and Japan;
(2) Russia, China, and the United States should not deploy any nuclear weapons in the area covered;
(3) Russia, China, and the United States should renounce permanently the use of weapons against non-nuclear states in the region on the condition that the states guarantee nuclear transparency and do not pose any nuclear threat against any state;
(4) The United States should maintain nuclear protection for South Korea and Japan against a nuclear threat from China or Russia, while China or Russia should provide the same protection for North Korea against a U.S. nuclear threat; and, most important,
(5) Non-nuclear states should not be subject to any restraints or disadvantages with regard to the non-military use of atomic technologies and facilities.

In addition to promoting a nuclear-free zone, Japan should take the lead in initiating an East Asian atomic cooperation organization in which atomic technologies and benefits therefrom would be shared, while sensitive materials would be collectively monitored and controlled by the member states. This would be a way to redress an unequal situation in which South Korea now forfeits opportunities for the development of its own atomic industry and is rendered virtually helpless vis-à-vis North Korea. Under the North-South denuclearization agreement of December 1991, pushed by the United States, both Seoul and Pyongyang are committed to forswear the development and use of reprocessing facilities for peaceful as well as military purposes. In the light of Japan's pursuit of reprocessing with U.S. approval, this agreement consigned Korea to a position of permanent inferiority in relation to Japan. As a result, the atomic industry of energy-poor South Korea is losing its vitality due to the absence of enrichment and reprocessing capabilities.

Unlike Japan, which disavows only the military use of atomic power, Seoul has limited its own economic potential by impeding and distorting even the peaceful use of atomic power. The establishment of a nuclear-free Korea will hinge, at least partly, on whether and how the surrounding countries help Korea to resolve this dilemma. It is in this context that Japan can and should lead both a multilateral atomic cooperation regime and a more aboveboard sharing of the peace dividends of the nuclear age. If, instead, Japan continues to pursue a unilateral technological edge, misgivings concerning its nuclear intentions will intensify in neighboring countries. The "South Korea That Can Say 'No'" might then be compelled to assert its own right to reprocessing capabilities, saying "No" not only to Japan but to the United States as well.

NOTES

[1]On January 9, 1994, then Secretary of Defense Les Aspin, appearing on ABC TV, indicated that North Korea may possess the bomb. On January 27, 1994, a Japanese weekly, *Jugan Moonchu,* reported that a group of Russian nuclear specialists argued in a report sent to Moscow that they believed North Korea already had one or two nuclear bombs. On January 20, 1994, CIA Director James Woolsey is believed to have told the Japanese foreign minister in Tokyo that North Korea had 16 to 20 kg of plutonium. *Dong-A Ilbo,* January 12, 1994; *Sege Ilbo,* January 27, 1994; *Chosun Ilbo,* January February 5, 1994.

[2]It brings to mind the fact that the mounting debate in Japan over theater missile defense and the Defense Agency's decision to consider beefing up its defenses against North Korean missiles came on the heels of Pyongyang's successful test of its new 1,000-km-range Rodong-1 in late May 1993. Also, Japan voiced similar distress at a Group of Seven summit meeting in July 1993 in opposing an indefinite extension of the Nuclear Non-Proliferation Treaty. The position was soon reversed, but many South Korean analysts saw it as an initiative to widen

Japan's latitude for a nuclear option for the future.

[3] Taifu Yu, "The Impact of the Cold War's End on Japan's Defense Policy," *Global Affairs*, Winter 1993, pp. 86-108.

[4] Thomas U. Berger, "From Sword to Chrysanthemum: Japan's Culture of Anti-militarism," *International Security*, 17:4, Spring 1993, pp. 119(50.

[5] Ibid, p.122.

[6] Peter J. Katzenstein and Nobuo Okawara, "Japan's National Security: Structures, Norms, and Policies," *International Security*, 17:4, Spring 1993, pp. 84(119.

[7] George Friedman and Meredith Lebard, *The Coming War with Japan* (New York: St Martin's Press, 1991).

[8] See, for example, Yoichi Funabashi, "Japan and the New World Order," *Foreign Affairs*, 70:5, Winter 1991/2, pp. 58(74.

[9] Op cit., Berger, p. 127.

[10] Op cit., Katzenstein and Okawara, p. 109.

[11] Op cit., Berger, p. 129.

[12] The exchange rate averaged 107 yen per dollar in April 1996.

[13] *KAIF* (Korean Atomic Industry Forum) newsletter, 104, May 11, 1993.

[14] Michael W. Donnelly, "Japan's Nuclear Energy Quest," in Gerald L. Curtis, ed., *Japan's Foreign Policy* (New York: An Eastgate Book, 1993), pp. 179–201.

[15] Taewoo Kim, Sungtaek Shin, and Minseok Kim. We tried to update Frans Berkhout, Tatsujiro Suzuki, and William Walker's excellent analysis of Japan's plutonium surplus, "The Approaching Plutonium Surplus: A Japanese/European Predicament," *International Affairs*, 66:3, July 1990, pp. 523–43 and Jinzaburo Takagi and Baku Nishio, "Japan's Fake Plutonium Shortage," *Bulletin of the Atomic Scientists*, 46:8, October 1990, pp. 36–38. For a more detailed analysis of Japan's plutonium capability, see Taewoo Kim and Minseok Kim, "The Korean Nuclear Question and Japan's Nuclear Policy," Bukhan Yonku (Study on North Korea), Autumn 1991, pp. 144–65.

[16] Korean Atomic Energy Research Institute, *Atomic Trends*, July 1992, pp. 85–86.

[17] Julian Steyn, "Uranium market braced for weapons material," *Nuclear Engineering International—Special Publications*, 1992, pp. 2–3.

[18] This refers to a nuclear armament process through which a nation, without revealing any military intention, proceeds to acquire all the elements of nuclear capability except for the possession of nuclear warheads themselves. For a definition of "asymptomatic," see George Quester, "Some Conceptual Problems in Nuclear Proliferation," *American Political Science Review*, 66:2, 1972, pp. 490–97.

[19] Malcolm McIntosh, *Japan Rearmed* (New York: St. Martin's Press, 1986), p. 64.

[20] For an analysis of the revisions to the U.S.–Japan Nuclear pact, see "US–Japan Nuclear Pact Draws Congressional Ire," *Science*, January 22, 1988, Vol. 239, p. 346; Frans Berkhout, Tatsujiro Suzuki, and William Walker, op cit., p. 535.

[21] *Asahi Shimbun*, February 18, 1994, reported that Japan would delay for twenty years the construction of a second nuclear-fuel reprocessing plant to avoid creating a domestic plutonium surplus. What the newspaper talks about, however, is in fact the third reprocessing plant, which is scheduled to be completed in 2010. The first plant was built in Tokai, and the second one is being constructed in Rokkashomura. Beyond this, according to Yoko Fukumoto of the *Mainichi Shimbun*, who inquired of the Science and Technology Agency at my request, the

issue of delaying the reprocessing project is currently under consideration in the broader context of the long-term atomic energy plan, which is to be revealed in the near future.

[22]For example, the U.S. Department of Energy canceled a recycling research cooperation program signed with Japan in 1993 for the reuse of plutonium. Nevertheless, the Japan Atomic Energy Research Institute continues research on plutonium treatment, including the active storage of plutonium, while governmental financing for the commercialization of MOX fuel by the year 2000 began as scheduled. See *KAIF* newsletter, 79, February 9, 1993; 189, February 18, 1994.

[23]For a detailed discussion of problems related to a nuclear-free zone on the Korean peninsula, see Taewoo Kim, "Fake and Reality of Nuclear-Free Korea," National Unification Board, *The Korean Journal of Unification Affairs*, 3:3, Autumn 1991, pp. 187–223 and "South Korea's Nuclear Dilemmas," *Korea and World Affairs*, Summer 1992, p. 254.

APPENDIX A

THE EXPLOSIVE PROPERTIES
OF REACTOR-GRADE PLUTONIUM

CHRISTOPHER E. PAINE

After a half century of living with nuclear weapons and seeking to prevent their proliferation, misinformation nevertheless persists regarding the amounts of fissile material required for nuclear explosive devices. Relative to other possible designs for single-stage fission weapons, a spherically symmetric implosion system requires the least amount of fissile material to achieve a given explosive yield and therefore represents the limiting case for assessing the proliferation threat and the effectiveness of safeguards. For this type of device, the amount of plutonium (or highly enriched uranium) required depends on the desired explosive yield of the device and the degree to which the fissile material is compressed at "explosion time" (the moment at which explosive disassembly of the fissile material begins due to the energy released by the exponential build-up of the fission chain reaction).

The degree of compression achieved depends on the sophistication of the design and degree of symmetry achieved by the imploding shock wave. There are, of course, other factors—such as the timing of the initiation of the chain reaction and the type of neutron reflector used—but for the purposes of this analysis, we will assume that the proliferant state or subnational group has already acquired the necessary skills from existing open sources or black-market transactions, so these factors are of secondary importance.

In figures A-1 and A-2, graphs show the explosive yield of a pure fission weapon as a function of the quantity of weapon-grade fissile material (weapon-grade plutonium in figure A-1 and highly enriched uranium in figure A-2) for three degrees of uniform compression. In the figures, the numerical factors of compression used in the calculations are assigned qualitative labels according to the relative technical sophistication of the designs; that is, whether they represent low, medium, or high technology. As seen from figure A-1, the Nagasaki bomb, Fat Man, which produced a 20-kiloton (kt.) explosion with 6.2 kilograms (kgs.) of weapon-grade plutonium (WGPu) falls on the "low-technology" curve. However, only 3 kgs. of WGPu compressed to the same extent would still have produced a 1-kt. explosion.

A 1-kt. yield is still an explosion with the potential to kill tens of thousands of people, depending on the population density and physical characteristics of the targeted area. Many tactical nuclear weapons that were in the U.S. nuclear arsenal had yields in the kiloton and even sub-kiloton range.

A-1. Yield vs. Pu Mass (as a function of technical capability)

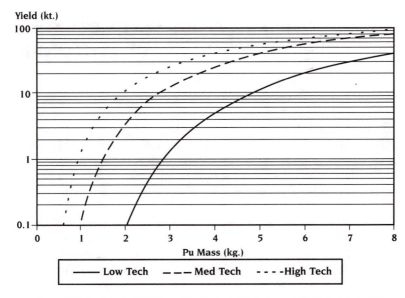

Source: T. B. Cochran and C.E. Paine, "The Amount of Plutonium and Highly Enriched Uranium Needed for Pure Fission Nuclear Weapons," *Nuclear Weapons Databook* monograph series, Natural Resources Defense Council, Washington, D.C., 13 April 1995.

A-2. Yield vs. HEU Mass (as a function of technical capability)

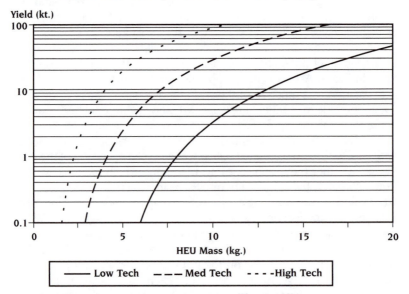

Source: T. B. Cochran and C.E. Paine, "The Amount of Plutonium and Highly Enriched Uranium Needed for Pure Fission Nuclear Weapons," *Nuclear Weapons Databook* monograph series, Natural Resources Defense Council, Washington, D.C., 13 April 1995.

But the bad news does not stop there. A non-nuclear weapon state today can take advantage of the wealth of nuclear weapons design information that has been made public over the past 50 years and do even better. As seen from figure A-1, to achieve an explosive yield of 1 kt. we estimate that from 1 to 3 kgs. of WGPu is required, depending upon the sophistication of the design. From figure A-2, we estimate that some 2 to 7 kgs. of highly enriched uranium (HEU) is required to achieve an explosive energy release of 1 kt. Table A-3 presents some of the results of our calculations in a different form. We estimate, for example, that as little as 2 kgs. of plutonium, or about 4 kgs. of HEU, is required to produce a yield of 10 kts.

Our calculations recently received independent, indirect corroboration from an unexpected source. Russia revealed in May 1995 that destruction was imminent for a nuclear-effects test device—originally placed in a horizontal tunnel at the Kazakh test site in May 1991—that contained "a total mass of almost 1 kg of plutonium" with a planned yield of "0.3 kilotons." These specifications are very close to those at the low end of the "medium-tech" and "high-tech" weapon design curves in figure A-1.

The curves in figure A-1 apply to WGPu where the Pu-240 content is less than 7 percent. Most of the plutonium in the civil sector is reactor-grade with a Pu-240 content in the range of 20–35 percent. However, the "prompt" critical mass of reactor-grade plutonium, irrespective of its Pu-240 content, will always fall between that of weapon-grade plutonium and HEU.

A brief digression on the differences between bombs and reactors will help explain why this must be true. The odd plutonium isotopes (239 and 241) are said to be "fissile"—meaning their nuclei can be fissioned by low-energy (so-called "thermal") neutrons that have been slowed by a "moderator," such as the water moderator–coolant in most civil power reactors. A reactor that relies on this thermal neutron spectrum takes advantage of the higher "cross section" of U-235 and Pu-239 atoms for fission by slow neutrons, allowing low concentrations of these materials (0.7

A-3. Approximate Fissile Material Requirements for Pure Fission Nuclear Weapons

Yield	Weapon-Grade Plutonium (kg.)			Highly Enriched Uranium (kg.)		
	Technical Capability			Technical Capability		
(kt.)	Low	Medium	High	Low	Medium	High
1	3	1.5	1	8	4	2.5
5	4	2.5	1.5	11	6	3.5
10	5	3	2	13	7	4
20	6	3.5	3	16	9	5

percent to 4.8 percent) to be used as fuel. The time required for the fast neutrons produced in fission to be slowed down, by non-fission, non-capture collisions with the moderator nuclei, introduces a lag in the growth of the chain reaction. This lag prevents the chain reaction from reaching explosive proportions before its own heat expands the fuel to "subcritical" density, shutting off the reaction.

Nuclear reactors have the further property that they are designed to achieve a self-sustaining chain reaction (called "criticality") in the fuel with the assistance of so-called "delayed neutrons," i.e., those that are not produced "promptly" by the fission reaction itself but rather in subsequent radioactive decay of some of the shorter-lived fission products. This affords a much longer time—on the order of minutes rather than microseconds—between neutron generations, allowing the power of the reaction to be regulated by withdrawal or insertion of neutron-absorbing control rods.

Nuclear explosives and the class of power reactors that also rely on a "fast- neutron" spectrum—so-called "fast reactors"—compensate for the lower-fission cross sections available at higher-neutron energies by using higher densities of chain-reacting material and a low density of neutron-absorbing materials. The isotopes Pu-240 and Pu-242 have a threshold for fission at neutron energies approaching one million electron volts (MeV), well above the thermal neutron spectrum used in most civil power reactors. Hence the origin of the (misguided) notion that Pu-240, the useless "non-fissile" isotope that builds up steadily with fuel exposure in a thermal reactor, might serve to "denature" the explosive properties of the plutonium produced in the spent fuel.

However, in a nuclear explosive the thermal neutron spectrum plays no role, and, unlike in a fast reactor, criticality and then an exponentially multiplying chain reaction ("supercriticality") is achieved in the fissionable material with prompt neutrons alone. The time between neutron generations is drastically reduced by the reliance on the prompt neutrons, leading to an explosive growth in the fission reaction. The average initial energy of a fission neutron, before collisions with other nuclei, is almost 2 MeV, and the average energy of a fission neutron moving in plutonium metal after a few "scatterings" (collisions), is about one MeV. For neutron energies above about 0.7 MeV, the fission "cross-section" of Pu-240 is smaller than that for Pu-239 but larger than that for U-235.

As Los Alamos weapons designer Robert Selden emphasized in a briefing to senior International Atomic Energy Agency officials in November 1976, "The most useful comparison of fissile materials for nuclear explosives is the comparison of fast neutron (prompt) critical masses" (emphasis added). Since the bare critical mass of Pu-240 as metal is about 40 kgs.—less than the 52 kgs. needed for a bare critical mass of weapon-grade uranium (94 percent U-235)—Pu-240 may be said to be a more effective fissionable material than weapon-grade uranium in a metal system.

"In practice," observes J. Carson Mark, former director of the Theoretical Division of the Los Alamos National Laboratory, "at all burn-up levels and at any time following discharge [from the reactor] the critical mass of reactor-grade plutonium metal is intermediate between that of Pu-239 and Pu-240, which is more reactive than weapons-grade uranium." He observes that "reactor-grade plutonium can be brought to a supercritical—and hence explosive—state, by any assembly system that can handle U-235." While this inconvenient fact has been studiously overlooked by the advocates of civil plutonium use, its relevance to the non-proliferation problem is beyond dispute.

Plutonium with a high Pu-240 content is less desirable for weapons purposes than WGPu, because, for low-technology weapon designs, the neutrons generated by the high rate of spontaneous fission of Pu-240 can increase the statistical uncertainty of the yield by initiating the chain reaction before the desired compression of the plutonium core has been achieved ("pre-initiation"). Also, the designers of such a weapon must take into account the extra heat generation and radiation exposures involved in using reactor-grade plutonium. In spite of these difficulties, militarily useful weapons with predictable yields in the kiloton range can be constructed based on low-technology designs with reactor-grade plutonium. According to the conclusions of a recent study by the U.S. National Academy of Sciences, based in part on a classified 1994 study by scientists at the Lawrence Livermore National Laboratory,

> even if pre-initiation occurs at the worst possible moment (when the material first becomes compressed enough to sustain a chain reaction), the explosive yield of even a relatively simple device similar to the Nagasaki bomb would be on the order of one or a few kilotons. While this yield is referred to as the "fizzle yield," a one kiloton bomb would still have a destruction radius roughly one third that of the Hiroshima weapon, making it a potentially fearsome explosive. Regardless of how high the concentration of troublesome isotopes is, the yield would not be less. With a more sophisticated design, weapons could be built with reactor-grade plutonium that would be assured of having higher yields.

By making use of various combinations of advanced technologies, including more rapid implosion techniques; using beryllium as a neutron reflector; and boosting the fission reaction with additional high energy (14 MeV) neutrons from deuterium-tritium fission and two-stage weapon designs, it is possible to offset the problems created by the high rate of spontaneous fission of Pu-240. As long ago as 1976, then Nuclear Regulatory Commission Commissioner Victor Gilinsky summed up the situation as follows:

> Of course, when reactor-grade plutonium is used there may be a penalty in performance that is considerable or insignificant, depending on the weapon design. But whatever we once might have thought, we now know that even simple designs, albeit with some uncertainty in yield, can serve as effective, highly powerful weapons—reliably in the kiloton range.

115

More recently, the Los Alamos National Laboratory released the following unclassified statement regarding the weapons-usability of reactor-grade plutonium:

Except for high purity Pu-238, plutonium of any isotopic composition, including that in spent fuel from commercial power reactors, can be used to make a nuclear weapon that is capable of significant nuclear yield. Design and construction of any nuclear weapon is a difficult task—but is a task that can be accomplished with a level of sophistication and computational capability that existed in the early 1950s at the nuclear-weapons design laboratories.

Examination of designs typical of 1950s nuclear weapons indicate that replacing weapons grade plutonium with plutonium of other isotopic composition could have two results: it might decrease slightly the maximum yield of the weapon, and it might reduce the probability that the maximum yield would be obtained in an explosion. However, even in extreme cases [i.e., involving high concentrations of Pu-240 and other non-fissile isotopes] yields on the order of kilotons would result [emphasis added].

NOTES

[1] Victor Litovkin, "Destroy Nuclear Device!" *Moscow Izvestiya*, May 23, 1995, p. 1.

[2] J. Carson Mark, "Explosive Properties of Reactor-Grade Plutonium," *Science and Global Security* 4 (1993): 115

[3] *Management and Disposition of Excess Weapons Plutonium*, Committee on International Security and Arms Control, National Academy of Sciences, National Academy Press, Washington, D.C., 1994 (Prepublication Copy), p. 37.

[4] Victor Gilinsky, "Plutonium, Proliferation and Policy," Commissioner, Nuclear Regulatory Commission, Remarks given at Massachusetts Institute of Technology, November 1, 1976 (Press Release No. S-14-76).

[5] Cited in Frank von Hippel, "Weapons-Usable Nuclear Materials Security after the Cold War," revised text of opening speech at a symposium at the Konrad-Adenauer House, Bonn, May 9, 1995, p. 4.

APPENDIX B

REACTOR-GRADE PLUTONIUM AND NUCLEAR WEAPONS

Excerpt from the Report of the U.S.–Japan Study Group on Arms Control and Non-Proliferation After the Cold War—from a section prepared by Working Group B on Asian Energy Development and Non-Proliferation, whose members are listed below—co-sponsored by the Carnegie Endowment for International Peace and International House of Japan. The Report is published as *Next Steps in Arms Control and Non-Proliferation* (Carnegie Endowment for International Peace, 1996).

The participants agreed that as a technical matter, with some additional efforts, a country can produce nuclear weapons using any kind of plutonium, using well-known technologies.

Japanese participants stated that the disadvantages of using reactor-grade plutonium in a production and in a military setting make it an unlikely candidate for weapon use by normal governments. They also stated that, for such a purpose, one would wish to have a set of warheads with reliable known yields and that one would also wish to have material that could be turned out in a production-line way.

There was agreement among the participants that international controls, such as International Atomic Energy Agency (IAEA) safeguards, should apply to any type of plutonium, since there is a possibility, however small, of using it to manufacture nuclear weapons. However, the participants agreed that additional international measures in addition to IAEA safeguards should be considered and proposed by the international community for deterring the diversion of plutonium to nuclear weapons.

Members of Working Group B

Hiroyoshi Kurihara *(Co-Chairman)*
Former Executive Director
Power Reactor and Nuclear Fuel
Development Corporation

Atsuyuki Suzuki
Professor of Nuclear Engineering
University of Tokyo

Victor Gilinsky *(Co-Chairman)*
Former Member
U.S. Nuclear Regulatory Commission

Makoto Ishii
Professor of Energy Economics
Azabu University

ABOUT THE AUTHORS

S ELIG S. HARRISON (Editor) is Director of the Carnegie Endowment Project on Japan's Role in International Security Affairs and served as a Senior Associate of the Endowment for twenty-two years. As a former Northeast Asia Bureau Chief of the *Washington Post,* based in Tokyo from 1968 to 1972, he closely observed the early stages of the ten-year Japanese debate over signing and ratifying the Nuclear Non-Proliferation Treaty. He is Adjunct Professor of Asian Studies at the Elliott School of International Affairs, George Washington University, and is the author of five books on Asian affairs and U.S. relations with Asia— including *The Widening Gulf: Asian Nationalism and American Policy and China, Oil, and Asia: Conflict Ahead?* In 1994 and 1995, he served as the U.S. Project Director of the U.S.-Japan Study Group on Arms Control and Non-Proliferation After the Cold War and was the author of its report, *The United States, Japan, and the Future of Nuclear Weapons.*

A TSUYUKI SUZUKI, Professor of Nuclear Engineering at Tokyo University, is Japan's leading academic specialist on nuclear fuel-cycle engineering. He served as a Research Associate in the Nuclear Engineering Research Laboratory of the University of Tokyo at Tokaimura from 1971 to 1974; as a Senior Researcher in the International Institute for Applied Systems Analysis, Laxenburg, Austria, in 1974 and 1975; and as a Research Associate and then Associate Professor in the Department of Nuclear Engineering, University of Tokyo, from 1975 to 1986, prior to his appointment as a full Professor. He is the author of *Nuclear Fuel Cycle Engineering, The Global Energy Path, and Plutonium.*

J INZABURO TAKAGI, Director of the Citizens Nuclear Information Center in Tokyo, is an influential critic of Japan's plutonium-based nuclear program. He is a graduate of the Science Faculty, Tokyo University, where he specialized in nuclear chemistry, served as a Research Associate at the University's Institute for Nuclear Study and received his Doctor of Science degree from the University in 1969. He has served as a researcher at the Nippon Atomic Industry Group, as an Associate Professor of nuclear chemistry at Tokyo Metropolitan University, and as a Guest Researcher at the Max Planck Institute for Nuclear Physics in Heidelberg, Germany. Dr. Takagi helped to found the Citizens Nuclear Information Center in 1975 and has served as its Executive Director since 1986. He is the author of numerous books in Japanese on nuclear chemistry and Japan's nuclear energy program. In 1992, he received the Yoko Tada Human Rights Award.

TAEWOO KIM, Senior Research Fellow of the Peace Research Institute in Seoul, is one of South Korea's best-known specialists on nuclear energy and non-proliferation and is a vocal advocate of an independent South Korean reprocessing capability. He is a former Senior Researcher of the Korea Institute for Defense Analyses and served as Director of its Nuclear Study Group. Dr. Kim received his Ph.D. from The State University of New York at Buffalo. He is the author of *South Korea's Nuclear Dilemmas, The Reduction of U.S.–Soviet Tactical Nuclear Weapons: The Impact on Korean and Global Nuclear Security; North-South Global Politics in Nuclear Diplomacy,* and other works.

THE CARNEGIE ENDOWMENT FOR INTERNATIONAL PEACE

The Carnegie Endowment for International Peace was established in 1910 in Washington, D.C., with a gift from Andrew Carnegie. As a tax-exempt operating (not grant-making) foundation, the Endowment conducts programs of research, discussion, publication, and education in international affairs and U.S. foreign policy. The Endowment publishes the quarterly magazine, *Foreign Policy*.

Carnegie's senior associates—whose backgrounds include government, journalism, law, academia, and public affairs—bring to their work substantial first-hand experience in foreign policy through writing, public and media appearances, study groups, and conferences. Carnegie associates seek to invigorate and extend both expert and public discussion on a wide range of international issues, including worldwide migration, nuclear nonproliferation, regional conflicts, multilateralism, democracy-building, and the use of force. The Endowment also engages in and encourages projects designed to foster innovative contributions in international affairs.

In 1993, the Carnegie Endowment committed its resources to the establishment of a public policy research center in Moscow designed to promote intellectual collaboration among scholars and specialists in the United States, Russia, and other post-Soviet states. Together with the Endowment's associates in Washington, the center's staff of Russian and American specialists conduct programs on a broad range of major policy issues ranging from economic reform to civil-military relations. The Carnegie Moscow Center holds seminars, workshops, and study groups at which international participants from academia, government, journalism, the private sector, and nongovernmental institutions gather to exchange views. It also provides a forum for prominent international figures to present their views to informed Moscow audiences. Associates of the center also host seminars in Kiev on an equally broad set of topics.

The Endowment normally does not take institutional positions on public policy issues. It supports its activities principally from its own resources, supplemented by nongovernmental, philanthropic grants.